How to Open & Operate
a Financially Successful

Cleaning

Service

With Companion CD-ROM

By Beth M.

How to Open & Operate a Financially Successful Cleaning Service — With Companion CD-ROM

Copyright © 2008 by Atlantic Publishing Group, Inc.
1405 SW 6th Ave. • Ocala, Florida 34471 • 800-814-1132 • 352-622-1875–Fax
Web site: www.atlantic-pub.com • E-mail: sales@atlantic-pub.com
SAN Number: 268-1250

ISBN-13: 978-1-60138-144-6   ISBN-10:1-60138-144-1

Library of Congress Cataloging-in-Publication Data

Morrow, Beth (Nancy Elizabeth), 1971-
  How to open & operate a financially successful cleaning service : with companion CD-ROM / Beth Morrow.
     p. cm.
  Includes bibliographical references and index.
  ISBN-13: 978-1-60138-144-6 (alk. paper)
  ISBN-10: 1-60138-144-1 (alk. paper)
  1. Buildings--Cleaning. I. Title. II. Title: How to open and operate a financially successful cleaning service.

  TX958.M67 2008
  648--dc22

                    2008024786

Printed on Recycled Paper

INTERIOR LAYOUT DESIGN: Vickie Taylor • vtaylor@atlantic-pub.com

Printed in the United States

THE HUMANE SOCIETY
OF THE UNITED STATES©

The human-animal bond is as old as human history. We cherish our animal companions for their unconditional affection and acceptance. We feel a thrill when we glimpse wild creatures in their natural habitat or in our own backyard.

Unfortunately, the human-animal bond has at times been weakened. Humans have exploited some animal species to the point of extinction.

The Humane Society of the United States makes a difference in the lives of animals here at home and worldwide. The HSUS is dedicated to creating a world where our relationship with animals is guided by compassion. We seek a truly humane society in which animals are respected for their intrinsic value, and where the human-animal bond is strong.

Want to help animals? We have plenty of suggestions. Adopt a pet from a local shelter, join The Humane Society and be a part of our work to help companion animals and wildlife. You will be funding our educational, legislative, investigative and outreach projects in the U.S. and across the globe.

Or perhaps you'd like to make a memorial donation in honor of a pet, friend or relative? You can through our Kindred Spirits program. And if you'd like to contribute in a more structured way, our Planned Giving Office has suggestions about estate planning, annuities, and even gifts of stock that avoid capital gains taxes.

Maybe you have land that you would like to preserve as a lasting habitat for wildlife. Our Wildlife Land Trust can help you. Perhaps the land you want to share is a backyard—that's enough. Our Urban Wildlife Sanctuary Program will show you how to create a habitat for your wild neighbors.

So you see, it's easy to help animals. And The HSUS is here to help.

The Humane Society of the United States
2100 L Street NW
Washington, DC 20037
202-452-1100
www.hsus.org

Table of Contents

Chapter 6: Organizing Your Business

Chapter 7: Human Resources

Chapter 8: Growing Your Business through Marketing

Foreword

By Perry D. Phillips, Jr.

There are countless books and Web sites on the market that tout home cleaning and maid service businesses as one of the "100 best small home businesses" or "best business to start for under $100" and most usually make claims of easy and big profits from the start. Do your homework; do not be fooled by these claims of a quick road to riches. Starting a home cleaning business is one of the easiest businesses to open. However, running, growing, and maintaining a sustainable, successful company in this industry can be quite a challenge.

Yes, it is true that you can start a legitimate home cleaning service for a very small upfront investment, especially if you intend to roll up your selves and do the work yourself, and do not mind doing it the hard way for quite a while. Building and growing a company, with all of the complex relationships, can be a daunting task even for the most seasoned of managers.

The Association of Residential Cleaning Services International (ARCSI) is pleased to see a resource like *How to Open & Operate a Financially Successful Cleaning Service* because it provides comprehensive information about not only how to get started, but what you can expect from the industry. I encourage you to take advantage of all learning opportunities available to you. Use these tools as you set goals for you and your new company.

Too often in this industry, individuals jump in, get started, and realize the reality of managing a financially successful business. This book along with the networking and educational opportunities ARCSI can offer will help you enjoy success in this challenging, but rewarding industry.

Along with the complex relationships and challenges you will face in this industry, the profit margin can be very rewarding financially, but you must run a tight ship. The residential cleaning industry as a whole is still very young compared to other industries. Professional, well-run residential cleaning companies have only been around for about 25 to 30 years. Demand from consumers continues to grow even in slow economic times. This growth is expected to continue to an all-time high for many years to come.

Good luck and much success in your new endeavor!

Perry D Phillips, Jr.
Founder and Executive Director
Association of Residential Cleaning Services International
www.arcsi.org
866.880.5914

ARCSI, the Association of Residential Cleaning Services International is the only non-profit organization that is dedicated to advancing the residential cleaning industry as a whole. Members are provided with incredible learning and networking opportunities. ARCSI's vision statement, "To Unify, Develop, and Promote the World's Most Successful Residential Cleaning Companies."

Introduction

There are two types of people who want to start a cleaning business: those who are driven by profits and those who are driven by passion.

While there is nothing inherently wrong with wanting to make a profit on your business, hundreds of people each year make the decision to venture into the cleaning industry based on the assumption that if they know how to clean, they should open a cleaning business to make quick, easy money. Upstart businesses like these rarely succeed due to one simple fact: a good cleaner does not necessarily make a good cleaning business owner.

Folks who are passionate about cleaning are willing to put in the long hours and do the hard work required to make owning a new business an exciting venture. They see that planning to reach their goals, taking action through research, learning about ownership, and building positive client relationships will serve their business for years to come. While it is true that anyone can clean, it takes a focused entrepreneur to start and grow a financially successful business.

Whether residential, commercial, carpet/upholstery, or a specialty/niche area, owning a profitable cleaning business comes with its own struggles and rewards. While you will spend a fair deal of time detailing the what, when, how, and why of what you want your business to accomplish, you will have the satisfaction of seeing your clients homes — and possibly lives — changed for the better as a result of your services. Starting a cleaning business from scratch is a bit intimidating if you have minimal background knowledge, but nothing is more gratifying than a referral call from a new client who heard about your services from a friend of theirs who was thrilled with your work.

If you are new to the cleaning industry, have done a bit of reading, or have just started a cleaning business and are looking to expand your knowledge — this book holds a wealth of information for building, enhancing, and strengthening your company:

- ✓ Traits of successful cleaning business owners

- ✓ Types of cleaning businesses

- ✓ Types of cleaning services

- ✓ Getting your business started

- ✓ Creating your business plan

- ✓ Creating your financial plan

- ✓ Startup capital, taxes, insurance

- ✓ Location strategies

- ✓ Organizing your office

- ✓ Recruiting, interviewing, hiring, and training employees

- ✓ Marketing, advertising, and customer-building

✓   Setting your fees to grow your company

✓   Cleaning techniques

✓   Interviews and insight from successful cleaning business owners

✓   Worksheets and samples to guide you through

From start to finish, all the details, insight, and business knowledge you need to get your company off the ground and build it into a success is packed in these pages. Beginning your venture with a foundation of knowledge, a desire to provide high quality service for a fair and reasonable price, and well-thought plans for growth are the first steps in creating a cleaning business that will stand the test of time.

Before You Begin

Maybe you first dreamed of owning your own business after a bad experience with an inconsiderate boss during your teenage years. Perhaps you enjoy managing others and the satisfaction of a job well done. Or maybe you find the challenge of creating a new business to meet customer needs an exciting prospect.

Whatever route you took through your life's journey to arrive here with an interest in establishing your own cleaning business, you have come to the right place. Full of opportunity, possibility, and potential, the cleaning industry is a profitable and exciting place to be.

From monthly house cleaning to daily office cleaning, the demand for quality, detail-oriented service providers outpaces availability. The range of reasons that bring new clients to the cleaning industry is consistently growing, and with it, the need for solid, reliable service at a reasonable and fair price. Consider the possible clients in these situations:

✓ A working couple with two young children who want to spend more time with their growing family than vacuuming and making sure the floors are spotless

✓ Baby boomers

✓ Aging people with reduced time, energy, or strength

✓ Free-time seekers

✓ Empty nesters interested in downsizing to smaller or single-level homes

✓ Janitorial staff that needs a helping hand

✓ Customers who want a thorough spring cleaning following the winter months

✓ A single person seeking a way to spend more time on a hobby or volunteer work

These potential customers provide a tiny representation of the variety of people in today's society who consider cleaning services an important part of their lives. Gone are the days of people viewing cleaning services from the traditional standpoint of being a luxury available only to the affluent. Whether a simple straightening and dusting or thorough office cleaning, modern cleaning services are becoming a way of life for more people. Common considerations steering new customers in the direction of hiring a cleaning service for their daily tasks include:

✓ Time saved

✓ Attention to detail

✓ Dislike of the tasks

✓ Affordability

✓ More leisure time

✓　Lifestyle changes (becoming sole caregivers of parents, late work hours)

✓　Dissatisfaction with current situation/help

These are the types of potential customers and the reasons they are hoping to find someone willing to give them the personalized, custom cleaning service they seek. You could be the person who can bring these customers what they are looking for in a cleaning service.

What Can You Expect?

Being your own boss, setting your own hours, being one of the major recipients of the profits of your business, and the prestige of being an entrepreneur and successful business owner are good reasons that may be driving you toward beginning your own business. Before we get too carried away with the fantasies, however, let us ground ourselves in something more specific: the daily reality of owning a cleaning business.

Setting the foundation for a cleaning business begins with weeks or months of hard work to solidify your business plan, establish service policies and offerings, research financing options, create and refine marketing strategies, develop hiring procedures, and familiarize yourself with all the legal aspects an entrepreneur needs to consider before opening for business. When faced with the reality of so many tasks to complete before you can even consider signing your first client, it is easy to become discouraged and overwhelmed. You might even consider giving up your dream at this point, but do not throw in the towel just yet. The good news is that despite the enormous list of things to do, these tasks may only have to be completed one time.

You would not take a vacation in an unfamiliar city without having a map to guide you on your adventure, and creating a business plan is no different. Aside from the need for potential investors to see solid evidence that you have thought through every aspect of your pending business, the peace of mind and security a well-conceived business plan provides for the business owner (you) and associates (your employees) is worth the hours it takes to create and refine. It does not make any sense to create a perfect menu of cleaning services your business will offer if you do not consider all varieties and avenues of advertising and marketing your services. Every solid, lasting, and profitable business began with a business plan. In Chapter 4 you will learn about the structure and elements you need to create a perfect business plan; using worksheets and detailed outlines, your business plan will come to fruition.

While others may not consider owning a cleaning service a glamorous, high-tech career, the potential for revenue and growth make it a lucrative field. You may not get the respect of big businesses, but after you gain the respect and loyalty of satisfied and loyal customers, you will have a solid base for building your business. Unlike numerous other businesses, the cleaning service industry is built on a high percentage of repeat customers using your service over an extended period. If you are able to provide service at a reasonable price, and if you pay attention to the customer's needs, you are almost assured profits from that customer. Think of it this way: Every single time you clean a customer's house or your janitorial staff services an office, there is no question that it will not last. You clean it, and it is guaranteed to get dirty again. The client will need it cleaned again in the future. If you have done a thorough job that meets their expectations, and they are pleased with your work, you will have the opportunity to do it again. One well-done job in the cleaning service industry may turn out to be the promise of more work in the future, so train your employees (or yourself) to care about the customer by offering your highest quality work, and you will reap the benefits.

Traditional occupations may depend on certain people to only deal with particular elements of a job, and those who begin the process may not get to enjoy the sense of exhilaration that comes with being able to see the positive effects of your progress. Cleaning offers that sense of completion where your progress is obvious and is evident to those around you.

Owning a cleaning business also provides a good profit margin. If you choose to begin with consumer cleaning — homes and other residential areas — you may already have the supplies and necessities in your cabinets and closets. Cleaning homes does not require any specific equipment to get started, though as your business grows you may consider purchasing equipment such as commercial grade vacuums with the ability to handle bigger jobs than regular consumer vacuums. Consumer-cleaning businesses may also work with the clients to get permission to use the appliances at that customer's house, eliminating the need to drag equipment from one house to another.

If consumer cleaning is not what you had in mind and you are more interested in establishing a commercial cleaning business, — janitorial services for offices, multi-unit buildings such as apartments, and office spaces — you still have a variety of options to choose from to limit your cost at startup. Commercial spaces may host their own appliances and may be willing to let you use them. You can also rent the equipment you need from local businesses, or you may be able to contract out a specific service your client requests. Each client brings a separate set of challenges and will have varied needs; starting small and working with customers on a one-on-one basis is a formula for success.

Is the Cleaning Business Right For Me?

Facing the realities of owning your own cleaning business is the first step in realizing what to expect on the business operational side, but that is only half of the story. Before you commit yourself to starting the cleaning business you have been dreaming of, consider the personal elements that come with starting your own cleaning business.

One consideration is the responsibility that comes with having so much decision-making power. While deciding that you want to open a cleaning business may seem simple on the surface, the reality is you have to be the one making the hard, fast choices that guide your business on a yearly, monthly, weekly, and daily basis. Making those crucial decisions requires more time devoted to research. You are in charge, and you have to base your decisions on solid reasoning because you will be the one your employees and clients come back to if your ideas do not work.

One of the initial choices you will have to make is the niche or focus of your business. More details of the types of cleaning businesses available as well as the types of cleaning services you can offer in Chapters 2 and 3, but you should stop and visualize for a moment where you are headed with your cleaning business. Are you more interested in cleaning homes and residential areas or businesses and offices? Does owning a franchise appeal to you, or are you planning to be independent? What services will you offer for your customers? How will your customer service go above and beyond what other cleaning services offer? Do you plan to expand your business in the future or keep it small? You will need to yourself these and other questions as you plan your business. Even if your dream is to own the biggest cleaning business in the word, you must start with the small, specific details that will guide your growth. You cannot be everything to everyone. Determining your niche is one of the first questions you need to answer on the way to establishing your business.

In the initial stages of business ownership — where your staff is small or non-existent — you will need to wear multiple hats. Being able to multitask and focus your attention in depth on one element of ownership at a time is a crucial skill you will need as your business grows. Your day may start with calling yesterday's clients to be sure they are satisfied with your service, or you may be balancing books and dealing with accounting issues. Training new employees might be your focus for a few hours, followed by meeting with vendors. While the types of jobs you can expect to do as the owner of a cleaning business may be the same jobs, no two days will be exactly alike. If there are parts of the job you do not enjoy, you will still have to perform them to the best of your ability to help your business run smoothly. After you have established yourself and are able to hire additional staff, you will be able to assign those duties and responsibilities to someone else. Until then you will be the one in charge of making sure you reach your business goals.

Another consideration is how you see yourself interacting in your business after you have a small successful client base. What is important is how you envision your involvement: cleaner, manager, or a little of both. You may begin a cleaning business because you love seeing progress or want to provide a high-demand, quality service but later discover after hiring several employees that you enjoy the management aspect of owning a small business even more. Or the opposite may be true; getting your hands dirty and making a difference through the quality of your work as you complete cleaning jobs might feel like the rewarding part of the job. The choice for how you divide your time is up to you, but you will need to think about it early on.

Which is more appealing to you: the social and interactive aspect of working with clients, vendors, and employees, or the solitary nature of losing yourself in a cleaning job? Your awareness of this preference can help guide you in choosing how you fit into the scheme of your business. The cleaning end is not completely silent — you will have to interact with customers and other team members as you service a job, but time spent talking casually is minimal since time equals money in the cleaning business. Though you will need to be cordial and friendly with clients if they are present during your cleaning, as a service professional you will need to keep your interactions brief so that you can focus your attention on the business of cleaning. If you find you prefer the relationship-building and networking aspect to the hands-on work, you may spend much of your day interacting through phone calls, e-mails, and personal visits to clients and others who are crucial to your business.

The success of any cleaning business is determined by the quality of your work. Outstanding interpersonal skills, hard work, dedication, and a fair price work to your advantage insofar as your cleaning services speak for themselves. Successful cleaning businesses, both consumer and commercial, are built on repeat business. These companies are built with as much as 90 percent of their business coming from repeat customers. The importance of quality service cannot be understated. Word-of-mouth advertising from satisfied customers to friends, family, and colleagues is powerful in terms of helping your businesses expand, and it is the best free publicity imaginable. Instill in your employees and yourself that nothing speaks louder and more positively about your services than quality work. Without it, your business will be just another listing in the Yellow Pages.

Stability and longevity are two aspects of owning a cleaning business that appeal to business owners. Since the best advice for growing your business is to take small steps and refine your service as you go, turning your business into the biggest company on the block will not happen overnight. Making a profit may happen in a shorter period, but using those profits to build for the future takes discipline and dedication. Cleaning services are not subject to big changes over time, but the changing needs of society combined with the integration of technology into every aspect of life does require the savvy business owner to stay abreast of changes in the service industry. Evaluating new ideas based on your needs and how they fit into your current services — selecting only those that meet your standards — is important to your success. It is important to have an interest in acquiring training as opportunities present themselves. Even within recent years, new niches have been created. Staying current with industry news, standards, and educational offerings can help your business prosper and keep up with the times.

Traits of Successful Cleaning Business Owners

Owning a successful cleaning business requires a host of skills and talents, and much of the success in your niche depends on how well you address the needs of clients seeking your service. New entrepreneurs may begin a cleaning business for two simple reasons: no special certification, advanced schooling, or degree is required, and if you begin small, you may already have the supplies and equipment you need to get off the ground.

Regardless of which type of business you start and what range of services you offer, there are a number of characteristics shared by successful operators in the business today. Successful owners are:

Time Managers

You need to make a commitment to put in the time and planning required to make a small business work. Your spare time and weekends will be filled with returning inquiries, providing estimates, and making contact with potential customers.

Dedicated

Promising and delivering a thorough cleaning job to your clients is a foundational belief of the cleaning service industry. There will be days you wake up and do not feel your best and find your schedule full of appointments. Canceling your appointments means canceling your paycheck. Rescheduling means disappointing — and possibly losing — customers who have come to rely on you. Realizing that your customers are the sole reason for the existence of your business and devoting the focus of your business to pleasing them is a guarantee for success.

Honest

You offer a service that brings you and your employees in daily contact with information that may be sensitive. Proving your trustworthiness to clients by ensuring their secrets are safe with you goes a long way in building rapport and boosts your credibility.

Professional

Maintaining a professional image will boost your company's credibility and make a favorable impression on clients. That attention to detail from you, your employees, and your vehicles, is one of the first visual representations of your business that the public and prospective clients will see. If you cannot pay the same level of attention and respect to yourself and your presentation, imagine how customers will interpret that as a direct relationship to the level of attention you will provide to their homes and businesses.

Organized

Whether you are looking for tax receipts for your accountant or trying to locate your feather duster, basic organizational skills are essential. No doubt you have heard the phrase "time is money," and when starting your own business, nothing could be more true. Knowing where to find things in a timely manner saves your sanity and gives you the advantage of being able to spend more time in other areas of your business.

"It is very important to always be prepared," shares Dan Johnson, owner of EnviroStat Professional Cleaning Services of Crossville, Tennessee. "To do this requires training, research, and a desire to succeed. If you are going to add services, learn the trade before offering it. If you are going to hire employees, research and know what your costs and liabilities will be. If you are going to make money, realize that taxes will be paid the following year, so make plans ahead of time how to earmark this money for that purpose."

Detail-Oriented

You may be under the impression that to own a cleaning business you need to love every aspect of housework, but that is not necessarily the case. What you do need to love is paying attention to the details of the job. Clients may not notice everything you clean, but they will notice what you do not clean. The importance of close attention to detail is also another argument for the value of starting small in the beginning. Start small, get every detail perfect, and then move upward.

Realistic

It is easy to get excited by the thought of raking in thousands of dollars a month in profit when you begin your own business, but tempering that with a little reality and common sense will serve you well as your business grows. Imagination and dreams are what lead every business owner to get started. Balancing that creativity with a shot of reality is what sets apart the dreamers from the entrepreneurs.

Friendly

Building relationships with your clients is integral to the success of your business. Knowing how to approach potential clients, assure current clients that their concerns are valid, and interacting on a professional, courteous level with employees and vendors requires strong interpersonal skills. While working alone may be the aspect of owning a cleaning business that appeals to you, without the ability to express yourself well and make those around you feel valued, your business will suffer. There are numerous books and programs to help strengthen your interpersonal skills if this is an area where you are uncomfortable.

Knowledgeable of Basic Business Skills

Your basic business knowledge will determine your ability to successfully establish and manage your business. Like interpersonal skills, basic business skills can be strengthened and improved through education. Local colleges, universities, and communities offer low-cost business classes for the beginner. You do not need a degree, but you do need foundational knowledge upon which to build your future.

Self-Knowledgeable

Knowing how and when to seek out help might seem a bit defeating, but wasting time on completing a task you know little about or are not trained to do is counterproductive to your business. Ask for help or hire assistance for things you don't know that you can be free to do the tasks you need to do and can do well. Being self-knowledgeable also includes knowing your limits and when to say "no" to a job, opportunity, or event if it does not fit into your mission or your plan.

For a helpful way to self-assess your skills and abilities as they relate to owning a cleaning business, see the Checklist of Necessary Skills worksheet in Appendix B.

Case Study: Alieen L. Johnston

Cinderella Housekeeping Services

156 E. Royal Forest Blvd., Columbus, OH 43214

614-261-0290

Aileen L. Johnston, Owner

ajohnsto@columbus.rr.com

Cleaners who become successful are cleaners who pay attention to every detail of the cleaning process. They bring that eye for detail into the business aspect of the cleaning business to make the company soar.

There are a multitude of ways to provide meaningful extras for employees and clients. For example, taking employees to lunch after an on-site training session, giving extra gas money for far-away jobs, and issuing Christmas bonuses encourage workers

Case Study: Alieen L. Johnston

to stay longer with Johnston, eliminating the "revolving door" employees that can worry customers. Likewise, something as simple as a background check on new employees reduces client uncertainty as well as protects the business. Johnston also keeps an eye on the local cleaning competition to make sure her rates are within a median range.

Making good on promises is a simple and effective way to ensure client satisfaction with any job. If they have a problem with their service, fix it. Johnston guarantees the quality of the cleaning services her employees perform. Earn client trust by having your phone calls forwarded from your business phone to a cell phone when you travel outside the office. There are no excuses for not taking every client relationship and concern seriously. Give them as much information as possible from the start of your relationship so they know what to expect, and deal honestly with them. One of the important details to mention is that as your business grows, the client will be paying for experience as well as service. Protect your reputation, and find genuine pleasure in dealing with people to get the most from your business.

Types of Cleaning Businesses

Now that you have more insight into the basics of owning your own cleaning business, here is a more complete picture of the types of cleaning businesses you may want to consider.

Consumer/Residential

Hundreds of people in your area come home exhausted after a long day of work and wish someone else could take care of cleaning their homes. Hundreds of others may enjoy cleaning home but have no time to get everything done. Hiring a consumer (or residential) cleaning service to help is quickly becoming a popular solution to dealing with these and other cleaning issues centered in the home.

Consumer cleaning services go beyond the commonly held notion of a maid. While maid service is one service a residential cleaning service can offer its customers, it is not the only one. Seasonal cleaning services, light cleaning, and heavy-duty cleaning are other possible services you can offer residential customers. A standard residential cleaning offers vacuuming, dusting, mopping floors, making beds, cleaning countertops, and wiping down fixtures. Chapter 3 provides in-depth information on residential cleaning and maid services.

The notion that only the rich and affluent can afford residential cleaning services is outdated. Working couples bring in dual incomes. Single people look for someone to take care of their cleaning needs while they devote their time to work or something they enjoy. Older clients seek help with chores they either no longer want to do or cannot complete on their own. These and other middle- and upper-income customers see the value in time savings of hiring someone else to do the work.

Residential cleaning services are not just limited to single-family homes. Managers of multi-unit buildings — apartments, condominiums, and duplexes — also need a reliable cleaning service between tenants. Homebuilders may be interested in having their model homes cleaned as they try to make a favorable impression on potential clients; they also need their newly-built homes cleaned after construction, prior to new families moving in.

If you want to get into the cleaning business by yourself, consumer cleaning services are the best place to start. You own much of the equipment and cleaning supplies you need to get started, and you can set your own schedule according to your needs. After you have a system down you will be able to add more homes to your rotation, and you will be able to complete numerous jobs in the same day. Successful residential cleaners work 40-hour workweeks and do their cleaning during the day while clients are at work, keeping their evening schedules open.

Benefits and drawbacks of residential cleaning services include:

✓ Residential cleaning jobs are manageable. You will not need to hire additional help in the beginning if you prefer to do the work alone.

✓ As your comfort level and knowledge of the job increases, so too can your number of daily clients.

✓ Your customer base is hundreds of thousands of possible customers. Anyone in a home, apartment, condominium, or duplex is a potential customer.

✓ Your customers may have the equipment you need for the jobs you will be completing for them. Additionally, you may have all the cleaners you will need on hand, minimizing your startup costs. Common household cleaners and equipment cost far less than industrial supplies and require no specialized training to use.

✓ You will have an opportunity to establish positive relationships with clients. If you do a good job, you will get free word-of-mouth advertising and more name recognition for you and your business with additional investment from you.

✓ There are clients who are never pleased no matter what steps you take to address their needs. You have to be careful in going too far to please the client if they continually want free additional services. Be firm but be fair. Your time is money.

✓ Your biggest competition can be the client who thinks they can do a better job than you can. Everyone has the ability to clean, so your service and attention to detail must be superior to what they can accomplish.

✓ While clients should be respectful of the cleaners who enter their home, they may harbor an attitude of superiority with hired cleaning staff. Outstanding residential cleaners come from a variety of backgrounds, including those who do not speak English as their first language. Regardless, they must be treated with respect. If the client cannot allow the cleaner to do their job without haughty behavior, it is best to end your relationship with that client.

✓ Clients who have little experience with cleaning services may have unreasonable or uncertain expectations and you may have to educate them.

Commercial

Commercial cleaning services are provided anywhere a residential/consumer-cleaning service is not: businesses, offices, hospitals, restaurants, retail establishments, and schools, to name a few.

The range of services you offer as a commercial cleaner is similar to what consumer cleaning services offer but on a larger scale. Vacuuming, dusting, mopping, cleaning common areas (such as break rooms, waiting areas, and administrative offices), restrooms, and lunch areas are standard services commercial clients need on a regular basis. You may also choose to add floor buffing, window washing, ceiling and wall cleaning, and carpet cleaning to your list of services after your business is established.

Commercial customers may have their own cleaning staff in-house, but that should not deter you for asking if you can be of service. There could be frequent jobs the in-house service needs to contract out or outsource. In addition, company cutbacks may have reduced the time employees can dedicate to janitorial duties. These potential clients have a deep desire for their establishments to be clean; they want to meet health and safety codes, impress clients, and provide a safe environment for their employees. It does not hurt to ask a potential customer if they might need your services even if they have their own janitorial staffs. Share your business card and contact information with them. If they do not need your service at the time you contact them, business changes may take place and they may open up their cleaning jobs to outside companies. Having made a pre-requisite contact, you could be the first one they call.

Unlike residential cleaning services where the work is completed primarily during normal business hours and clients are away or at work, janitorial services tend to do their work after-hours. Clients may want your service during the day, but numerous customers will prefer you come after their employees and customers have gone for the day.

Even the smallest commercial job is bigger than any consumer job. Where you may be able to clean several homes in one day, commercial janitorial jobs are larger jobs. Janitorial work is not recommended for individuals; instead, teams of cleaners visit one setting and complete all the tasks contractually agreed upon. If your strength lies in scheduling and management, janitorial service may be a good place for you to begin.

Here are additional considerations for starting a commercial cleaning service:

✓ Even businesses with in-house cleaning staffs may be able to use one component of your services.

✓ You can custom-tailor your janitorial services to meet the needs of your clients. For example, clients may want only certain jobs performed, or they may need daytime janitors instead of night crews.

✓ Supervisors direct your cleaning teams as you set them up, freeing your time for office, management, administrative, and customer service tasks.

✓ If you begin small and offer only services you have the equipment and supplies for, your initial expenses will be substantially lower.

✓ A quality job is its own calling card. If you focus your services in the commercial arena, your work will be viewed by more people and can be a free way of networking for future business clients.

✓ Commercial clients may have needs that require specialized equipment, such as carpet scrubbers and buffing machines, which may require trained personnel to operate.

✓ Janitorial services are not the glitziest jobs in the world, but they are full of potential clients and possible profits.

✓ The job may be too much for one individual to accomplish in one day.

✓ Employees are expected to work evening shifts and may work through until morning to complete a job.

✓ Because of the quantity of supplies you will need, initial janitorial supply costs will be greater.

Though the fields of consumer and commercial cleaning businesses offer customers different services based on their needs, there is no reason your business cannot offer services to both. If you are interested in servicing both types of clients, you will want to start small and narrow your focus doing several jobs well before looking toward expansion. You may have big aspirations, but until you can prove yourself on a small scale, there is nothing to back your claims to potential customers.

Independent

As an independent cleaning business owner, everything about your business, from logo design to services you offer to your billing system is yours responsibility. You will build your business from the ground up. Every choice is up to you.

As an independent business owner, you get to select and choose the services you want to provide. If you do not like window cleaning, for example, you can offer it as an additional option to your basic residential services. If you prefer to work only on Wednesday mornings, you can arrange your appointments accordingly.

Advantages and disadvantages of establishing your business as an independent owner:

- ✓ You will determine your market niche based on what you like to do, what you do well and what you see a need for. You have the flexibility to add, change, and eliminate elements of your business as you see fit.

- ✓ Nothing is prescribed. From the color of your uniforms to the size of the advertisement you list in the paper, each component of your business can be custom-designed to reflect your business to the public.

- ✓ Profits are all yours. The money you earn as an independent business owner can be put back into growing your business. In franchises, your business keeps only a percentage of the profits while the rest go to the parent company.

✓ Starting from scratch requires much less startup money. While buying a franchise costs upwards of $15,000 for the basic franchise fee alone, you can become an independent cleaner using minimal products and equipment you may already have on hand.

✓ You determine the speed at which you grow. Franchises have expectations of how many services you must provide from the start, but if you are in control, you can start small and add services as you grow.

✓ The investment of time dedicated to planning and researching your independent cleaning business prior to implementing your services is longer.

✓ To know your market, customers, sales, and market trends, you will need to do research regularly.

✓ Where is no name recognition when you first get started. Customers will only know you by your advertising, references, and word-of-mouth advertising. Building a customer base as an independent cleaner takes time, patience, and attention to detail.

✓ You are responsible for all marketing and publicity for your business. You will need to create a logo, develop a mission statement, and get yourself listed in the Yellow Pages and local business directories.

✓ The only way to learn the right and wrong ways to operate an independent cleaning business is by doing. Mistakes take time to remedy, but trial and error you will learn. There are no guidelines to follow in establishing an independent cleaning business. You create the guidelines.

Startup Businesses

Startup cleaning businesses are a type of independent cleaning business. As the name suggests, startups are created from the ground up. You have every say in what goes into your business, how you operate, and what services you offer. A startup business is yours alone.

Starting your own business has benefits, such as:

- ✓ You define your business your way. There are no expectations to follow outside of what you create.

- ✓ Hidden legal issues and potential dangers and problems are of no concern. You are aware of everything from the start, and you will not be taken by surprise.

- ✓ Staff and clients are hired and signed by you.

- ✓ You can start small and grow as your confidence, abilities, staff, schedule, and client list grow.

- ✓ The image and foundation of your business is your own creation. Clients will get to know your business as a reflection of you, your goals, and your integrity.

- ✓ You have yourself to blame if you hire poor employees.

- ✓ Servicing and cleaning for clients happens after you have established, planned, and prepared the business portion of your cleaning business.

Established Businesses

Established businesses are cleaning businesses already in operation that are being sold by the current owners. Finding a cleaning business for sale is easy. You will see listings in your local paper, trade publications, business brokers, and online. You may be able to purchase the business and all the equipment, office supplies, and customer accounts that go with it.

Before deciding to purchase an existing cleaning business, you need to put in the time and energy to research and develop your business plan as if you were starting your own business. You need to see the records, books, and account information for the business and examine the fine print of the contract of sale from the current owners. There may be details you agree to follow by signing the contract that you need to be aware of. Involve your lawyer and accountant prior to signing any contract for an existing business to give you solid footing. If you choose to investigate the business for possible problems, maintain a low profile and use common sense to avoid causing undue problems with the business. Most important, establish a positive, professional relationship with the current owners to gain their full cooperation in assuming leadership of the business to maintain consistency of service for customers during the transition period.

While taking over an existing cleaning business eliminates a fair amount of the groundwork required to start your own business, there are other things to consider before such a purchase. These include:

- ✓ Clients and cleaning staffs are already in place, giving you an opportunity to assume a leadership position immediately.

- ✓ Good vendor relationships are established.

- ✓ Zoning and permit requirements have been filed. Business paperwork has been completed and recorded.

✓ Initial market research is done and will only need annual updates.

✓ The business has established its niche for customers. You may decide to expand the niche to offer additional services or leave the niche as it is.

✓ With an established business, changes may be difficult to implement. Customers may have specific expectations, and altering those might send the clients to another service.

✓ With a new management style and focus, current employees face uncertainties with you replacing the previous employer. They may have talents you need time to recognize; they may also provide challenges to your leadership style that were not issues with the previous owner.

✓ As the business is experiences a management turnover, so will the client base. It will take time and to either re-establish those clients or increase the business so that the loss of those client accounts does not affect your bottom line.

✓ Though much of the work in establishing the business has been done for you, it will take time to learn the business in-depth. You may be unpleasantly surprised by unmentioned legal or staff work issues that require time to remedy.

✓ Starting small is impossible. Scheduling clients and staff, maintaining records, accounts, and vendor contracts, and the hustle and bustle of daily office activities may be too much at the start if you have little or no experience with managing daily operations.

Franchise

Starting a cleaning business from scratch can be an intimidating prospect. Instead of establishing an independent business, anxious entrepreneurs may choose to pursue franchise ownership.

Owning a franchise can be as simple as choosing which franchise best reflects the type of company you would like to work for, applying for a franchise with that company, and raising the required start-up cash to buy into the franchise. Franchises may also require you to go through interviews and evaluations; they want to make certain you are a good fit for their company's mission and goals. If you are interested in pursuing franchise ownership, thoroughly examine and research all aspects of that franchise's operations.

Franchises can be national or regional in scope. Nationally based franchises may work on a regional level as well. Franchises work with you on all aspects of your business from the minute you begin. They provide all the paperwork, guidance, rules and policies, expectations, and marketing you will need to get your business up and running. The most you may have to do is hire employees for your business.

If you are thinking about a franchise, consider these observations before you make your final decision:

- ✓ Franchise ownership means everything is laid out for you. Procedures, expectations, services, legal considerations — everything you need to think through prior to implementation of your business — is done for you. All you will need to do is put their plans into action.

- ✓ Research is updated regularly. From marketing trends to new, improved ways of cleaning, you will not need to take time from your business to track changes.

✓ Franchises have strong name recognition. You will spend less time building your reputation than if you started from scratch.

✓ Marketing and advertising with a franchise reaches regional and national customer bases. Local customers will be familiar and comfortable with your business's name from the start.

✓ Customer satisfaction has been studied from all angles in a franchise. Today's franchise information is built on a history of learning from past mistakes, and the guiding documents of franchises reflect this.

✓ Franchise ownership is expensive and does not necessarily guarantee large profit. You keep only a royalty, or percentage, of your business's profits.

✓ Being told what to do, how to do it, and guided by franchise expertise may be helpful and appealing at the onset of your business, but as your business grows and expands, your hands are tied. Franchises expect you to follow their guidelines right down to the tiniest detail. While this ensures a consistent image and service for the franchise, it eliminates any chance for your own creativity and ideas to flourish — even if you find a better way to service your customers.

✓ Company changes at the top are expected to be implemented all the way down the line to your customers. You may be required to alter a policy or service that can negatively affect your client relationships.

✓ If another franchise within your parent company experiences legal issues, customer problems, or negative press, this may affect your business as well. Despite the fact that individual businesses beneath a parent company's umbrella are independent franchises, negative name recognition from one franchise operation may unfairly influence yours.

✓ Franchises may require independent businesses to purchase things like cleaning solutions, equipment, and uniforms from preferred vendors. You may be able to get a better price from other vendors or suppliers, but in signing a contract with a franchise, you must adhere to their specifications and guidelines.

For help in choosing the business type that best meets your needs, see the "Choosing Your Business Type" worksheet in Appendix B.

Case Study: Mona Makela

Heavenly Maid Cleaning Service, Inc.

Gresham, OR

www.heavenlymaidcleaningservice.com

Mona Makela, owner

Doing your homework before starting a cleaning business is a necessity. If you have a local small business development center, they can help develop strategies to improve your business, assist in writing a business plan, and offer counseling and workshops. Find out what city, state, and county documents you are required to submit as well as local licensing requirements if you are a home-based business owner.

Put the same thought into what types of products, equipment, and services you will offer. Different services require different equipment. Residential and general office cleaning are often the easiest and least expensive places to begin and require the least amount of start-up cash to establish.

Case Study: Mona Makela

Having references for your services is important. If you need to offer a free cleaning or two or discount your services, be sure you have at least three satisfied references potential clients can call to ask about the quality of your services.

Put the time into training your employees so they are well-versed and thoroughly educated with your cleaning techniques and expectations before they service clients. It is helpful to have an "in-house" trainer to do the training sessions until both parties feel comfortable with the new hire going to a job site on their own.

Be grateful for your customers, and make your employees happy. A happy cleaner makes for a happy customer, and without them you will not have a business.

Types of Cleaning Services

Building your business from scratch is an exciting adventure full of decisions, options, and infinite possibilities. The creative stage — where choices determine the foundation and lay the groundwork for your future business — may be the most thrilling and intense. No doubt you have ideas brewing in your mind about the world of cleaning businesses and all it has to offer. In this chapter we will examine the different types of services your business (whether independent or established, consumer or commercial) can be built on and offer your customers.

Residential Cleaning Services

Maid Service

Ask working couples, women who work outside the home, busy singles, and even stay-at-home parents what they would like most in their day and you will hear responses such as "more time," "time to relax," and "time to myself." Time in today's society is becoming a valuable commodity, which makes maid service a more crucial — and lucrative — business.

What It Is

Maid service, in all its varieties, boils down to one thing: housecleaning inside a manageable space. The low startup costs and high sales potential, along with limitless customer base, make it a perfect starting point in the cleaning service industry that you can begin from your home.

Maid services clean more than just homes. Immediately consider single-family homes, apartments, and condominiums as potential customers. After a maid service is established and confident in their cleaning abilities and approaches, they may branch out to include clients such as rental homes, apartments between tenants, model homes, and new construction homes after the builders and installation crews are finished before the buyers move in. Even in multi-unit residential dwellings, such as condominiums and apartments, there are numerous opportunities to clean on a smaller scale when you consider common areas that need servicing: offices, workout rooms, restrooms, laundry rooms and clubhouses.

Maid services may have several cleaners/teams on staff, and as the owner you will spend your time on administrative and office tasks like customer service, scheduling, maintaining and ordering supplies, contacting potential customers, payroll, and billing, while your crews handle the actual cleaning.

What You Will Do

Just because you are a maid service does not mean you will clean everything from top-to-bottom within a home or small office. Customers have different needs for your services. Clients may want only light cleaning: vacuuming, dusting, wiping down countertops and cabinets, making beds, and removing trash. Other clients will hire you for more heavy-duty tasks including scrubbing floors, toilets, sinks and showers, mopping, baseboard cleaning, and others. While you will offer a standard service to customers, tailoring your services to meet their needs is what will build your reputation and relationship with that customer.

Basic maid services include:

- ✓ Whole-house cleaning

- ✓ Dusting (furniture, blinds, televisions, fixtures)

- ✓ Making beds

- ✓ Vacuuming floors, drapery, furniture

- ✓ Polishing furniture

- ✓ Scrubbing tubs, showers, sinks, and faucets

- ✓ Cleaning mirrors, floors, telephones, light switches, and door handles

- ✓ Removing trash

- ✓ Kitchen cleanup

- ✓ Wiping down cabinets, countertops, cupboards, appliance exteriors, and microwave interiors

- ✓ Dusting tops of cabinets

- ✓ Cleaning countertops and sinks

In addition to these common services, you may choose to offer other services to customers for which you can charge an additional fee. These may include but are not limited to the following:

✓   Whole-house cleaning

✓   Washing walls and windows

✓   Changing bed and bath linens

✓   Cleaning fireplaces, windowsills, baseboards, doors, and frames

✓   Strip, wax, and buff floors

✓   Oil and polish woodwork

✓   Kitchen

✓   Cleaning the refrigerator

✓   Defrosting the freezer

✓   Oven and stove top cleaning

What You Will Need

A specific equipment and procedures for residential cleaning is provided in Chapter 11, but for now here are there are common necessities for getting your maid service started. You first have a decision to make: Do you prefer to use the cleaning supplies and equipment your customers already have and use in their own homes, or do you want to bring your own? As a new business owner, you may want to use your clients' materials to save money. Clients may even prefer you use the cleaning supplies they are comfortable with. In addition, you will save time and energy not having to carry your equipment and cleaning solutions from one job to another.

You may, however, want to use products and equipment that you know from experience do the best job and bring them on your own. You will know you have enough products to finish the job, and you can organize your products so they are easy to locate, thus saving you time. Familiarity with the products will save time learning proper usage techniques, and you can choose ecologically friendly, hypoallergenic, super-strength cleaners your customers may not be able to purchase. You may be able to buy cleaning solutions in bulk from wholesalers and mix them with water for a lower cost. Moreover, having your own equipment and products strengthens your professional image. The choice is yours based on the needs of your business and your customers — who should have the final say in what you use in their homes.

After you have decided, here are common guidelines on the products and basic cleaning equipment you will need to do a thorough job.

Basic Cleaning Products

Every cleaning job will need:

- ✓ Mild, all-purpose cleaner for countertops, cabinets, and faucets — spray bottles recommended

- ✓ Disinfectant cleaner for kitchens and bathrooms

- ✓ Mild abrasive cleaner for sinks, showers, and countertops

- ✓ Heavy-duty abrasive cleaner for tile

- ✓ Glass cleaner for windows, appliances, and televisions

- ✓ Wood cleaner for furniture, cupboards, baseboards, and wood floors

- ✓ Furniture oil for select furniture jobs

- ✓ Dusting spray for dry mops and cleaning cloths

✓ Dish detergent/soap-based solution

✓ Degreaser

Basic Equipment

You will need the following equipment for cleaning:

✓ Upright vacuum for carpeted floors

✓ Canister vacuum for stairs, upholstery, and drapery

✓ Dust mop

✓ Sponge mop

✓ Cotton mop

✓ Broom and dust pan

✓ Paper face masks

✓ Squeegee

✓ Eight to ten cleaning cloths per job

✓ Duster with extension for reaching ceilings

✓ Rubber gloves

✓ Bucket

✓ Extension cord for each vacuum

✓ Hand/stiff-bristle brush

✓ Spray bottles

Like cleaning products, specialty or additional cleaning service jobs you offer to customers may require special equipment.

Downsizing Services

People from all walks of life have become dissatisfied with their current lifestyle of "having it all." Whether for sociological or ecological reasons or in the interest of practicality, people are choosing to downsize their living arrangements. Residential cleaning services, with a basic organizational mindset and attention to detail, can use their existing services to capitalize on this growing business.

What It Is

Downsizing appeals to a variety of clients. The aging population in our society, such as empty nesters, baby boomers, and retirees, are finding a need to move from larger homes, offices, and lifestyles into smaller living quarters. For these clients, their current possessions, furniture, and other items do not fit into their relocation plans.

What You Will Do

As a downsizing specialist, you will serve as a consultant and service provider to your clients. Your first task will be to assess the size of the job. The components of the service are easy: taking inventory of and then helping to organize, pack, and clean before the client's move. You will also help determine what items need to go into a storage facility and what possessions to keep, donate, or throw away. Responsibility for contacting the junk/waste removal companies, the storage facility, and possible charities for donation may also be a part of your service. Multiple client visits will be required, along with an ability to focus on the ultimate goal and meticulous organizational strategies.

Elements of a downsizing service include:

- ✓ Thorough cleaning of the current residence during the process of reorganization and after the client has moved

- ✓ Grout and tile cleaning

- ✓ Painting and restoration of walls and baseboards

- ✓ Carpet and floor cleaning, mopping, and waxing

- ✓ Duct cleaning

- ✓ Fireplace maintenance

- ✓ Appliance maintenance and cleaning

- ✓ Cleaning the future residence prior to moving in, if necessary

- ✓ Helping the client move items to the storage facility and donation centers

- ✓ Assisting in unpacking and organizing items at the new residence

What You Will Need

Part of the appeal in offering customers downsizing services is that as an established maid/residential service you will use many of the same products and equipment you already have on hand. The major difference will be the investment of time to the job. Instead of finishing five or six traditional cleaning jobs in one day, you may spend several days or even weeks working in-depth with your client.

The jobs you need to perform with your downsizing service you may be able to accomplish with your current cleaning teams. If not, you may wish to consider qualified subcontractors that you trust will do a thorough, professional job that will enhance your business image and credibility.

In addition to basic products and services, you will need staff members who have superior organizational skills, respect for client property, the energy and ability to handle larger projects, and are comfortable working closely with clients over an extended time. They should also have excellent interpersonal skills to build solid, trusting relationships with their customers. For this reason, you may want to choose a more mature staff member. Knowing the strengths of your cleaning employees will guide you in making this decision.

Estate Cleaning

Employees with strong relationship-building skills are also assets if you choose to branch out into the world of estate cleaning. When clients hire a service for estate cleaning, there may be more emotion and concern involved than in the typical maid service weekly or biweekly cleaning. Customers may not remember all the services you offered to them as an estate cleaner, but they will remember the compassion with which your staff treated them at this time in their lives.

What It Is

Estate cleaning services take place in a residence after a person is deceased. Families may contact you from out of town or out of state to take care of the estates of their parents with minimal input or to assist them on the premises. Like downsizing, estate cleanings are more time-intensive and may take days or weeks to complete.

What You Will Do

Estate cleanings take place to ready possessions for an estate sale. Sorting possessions from trash, cleaning items and the home, and preparing for the sale itself are common estate cleaning services.

The actual home cleaning tasks your crews will perform are the same as maid and downsizing services. Clients may want a complete and thorough house cleaning or they may only want minimal services. As clients are routinely the adult children of the deceased, they may have special requests for servicing items, such as storing and packing valuables and cherished possessions for safe storage or for shipping to other family members in different locations.

What You Will Need

The supplies and equipment may be the same ones you have on hand from other jobs. In instances where consumers want every nook and cranny of the home cleaned, your best bet is to subcontract to qualified service providers those jobs you and your staff are either not comfortable with, not certified or trained to do, or that require specialized, expensive equipment to properly complete.

Employees you select to represent your business for estate cleaning services should be patient, attentive and caring. In addition to selecting a trusted employee who is capable of performing physical cleaning tasks, clients may still be in the grieving process and require compassion and kindness from your employee, so select carefully. You may need to adjust the pay of the workers you choose to serve as estate cleaning specialists to reflect the level of personal service they give the client rather than the amount of work or jobs they complete.

Seasonal Cleaning

Season transitions — winter to spring, summer to fall, spring to summer, and fall to winter — are common times for people to take inventory and stock of their current living conditions. These are prime opportunities for your business to offer additional services to clients who need an extra hand in completing these chores. Seasonal cleaning services may be more heavy-duty and, as a result, command a higher price.

What It Is

Seasonal cleaning is exactly as its name implies: cleaning homes during transitional periods throughout the year. Clients have a variety of needs and tasks they want to complete around their home, and may lack the time, energy, or physical ability to complete those tasks on their own. They may only want a more detailed interior cleaning, dusting, and vacuuming service, or they may need windows detailed, carpets cleaned, floors waxed and buffed, or silverware polished.

What You Will Do

Your company's seasonal services will not only be determined by what your crews can handle or you want to offer, but by what customers want. Seasonal cleaning chores can include:

- ✓ Carpet cleaning

- ✓ Wall and baseboard cleaning

- ✓ Drapery and curtain cleaning

- ✓ Window cleaning and window sill detail

- ✓ Storm window removal or installation

✓   Ceiling, corner, and cobweb cleaning

✓   Upholstery and furniture cleaning

✓   Removal of trash and clutter

✓   Possible restoration work from water damage

✓   Chimney cleaning and preparation services

✓   Silverware polishing

What You Will Need

Based on the services you offer, you may be able to complete these tasks with your current staff. You may need to dedicate more time to jobs that are more intensive in nature, such as upholstery cleaning and window cleaning. If your crew is hired to do a seasonal cleaning, you may want to limit their schedule that day to focus on completion of only that task.

In terms of equipment and supplies, seasonal cleaning jobs can be accomplished with the inventory your regular maid services have. Working with the client and basing your services on their needs, you may be asked to do a job you are either not prepared or not equipped to complete. In this case, you may be able to rent the equipment (steam cleaner or floor buffer, for example) to complete the job yourself, choose to purchase the equipment if you have a number of customers requesting the same service, or subcontract that task to reliable professionals.

Carpet and Upholstery Cleaning

Although cleaning carpets and upholstery — from drapes to furniture coverings to accessories around the home — is listed as a consumer service, it also falls into a commercial service.

What It Is

With the introduction of wall-to-wall carpeting came the need for that carpeting to be cleaned. Traditional vacuuming on a regular basis removes the loose dirt on the surface of the carpet, but to clean carpets and other fabrics, a deeper treatment is necessary. Carpet and upholstery cleaners use special equipment to lift and remove soil, stains, and other debris from inside the carpet or fabric using water or chemicals, depending on the process you choose.

Residential clients may use a carpet and upholstery cleaning service on a semi-annual or seasonal basis. Businesses may choose a more frequent basis since they have higher foot traffic than a home or residence.

A cleaning business may offer carpet and upholstery services exclusively or it may just be an additional service. If you find a number of your clients requesting the service, you could consider investing in the equipment and supplies to broaden your customer base.

If you choose to specialize in carpet and upholstery cleaning, there are other services you can offer your clients, including:

- ✓ Wall and ceiling cleaning

- ✓ Fabric protection

- ✓ Carpet dyeing and restoration

- ✓ Spot and stain removal

- ✓ Smoke and fire damage cleanup and restoration

- ✓ Water damage restoration

✓   Flame-retardant treatments

✓   Odor and humidity control

✓   Cleaning, restoration, and maintenance of other flooring materials, such as hardwood, laminate, stone, and tile

What You Will Do

Upholstery

Depending on the type of fabric and fiber composition of that fabric, upholstery may be cleaned with the same equipment you use for shampooing or dry-cleaning carpets. You will need additional attachments for the equipment to service the upholstery properly, or you can purchase specialty machines designed to clean upholstery and drapery. Following every upholstery cleaning, you will want to protect the furniture against future stains by treating the upholstery with a fabric protector.

Carpets

You will need to do a bit of research on what your customer wants from your service before employing one of three standard methods. While the industry is divided on which cleaning method is the best, each has it merits and drawbacks.

Prior to whichever carpet cleaning method(s) you employ, you will want to use a stiff brush to loosen soil. Use a pre-conditioner on the carpet pile and use a high-powered vacuum to remove remaining dirt and debris. Following each carpet service, application of a fabric protector such as Teflon® is recommended to extend the life of your service.

After you have determined the needs of your client, you will use one of the following methods to clean carpets:

Wet Shampooing

Wet shampooers work by applying detergent and water to the top carpet fibers and using rotary brushes to work the detergent in. Then a wet pickup extractor is used to remove the loosened soil and moisture.

Rotating brush machines are available at department stores, but these machines are not durable enough to withstand the demands of repeated, high frequency use. You can rent or purchase more powerful equipment, but wet shampooing is the least favored of the three methods. In addition to the belief that the brushes only drive the dirt deeper into the pile, it can take five days to completely dry.

Steam Cleaning

Also known as "deep soil extraction," the use of the word "steam" in steam cleaning implies hot steam is used to clean carpets. Instead, steam cleaning is a high-powered version of wet shampooing without the use of rotary brushes. The application of high-temperature steam to a carpet can damage materials or cause the fabric to shrink.

Like wet shampooing, steam cleaning involves spraying a detergent and hot water solution on the carpet. The difference from wet shampooing is that the water is heated to about 150 degrees, forced into the pile via controlled jet streams, and then immediately extracted by a powerful vacuum.

Steam cleaning is a common method of carpet cleaning in residential homes. Businesses with high traffic areas may be better served with shampooing to loosen more ground-in dirt than steam cleaning. Practice your steam cleaning method prior to servicing clients to avoid over saturating carpet with water. Unlike shampooed carpets, steam cleaned carpets may be dry in two to six hours.

Chemical Dry Cleaning

Despite the notion that dry cleaning is moisture-free, this method of carpet cleaning involves spraying carpet with a carbonated chemical that breaks down soil. Next, the carpet is buffed with a pad to pick up the dirt and surface soil.

Chemical dry cleaning requires a strong vacuum to finish the process; otherwise, the grit and sand that grinds down fibers can remain behind and affect the life of the carpet. The dirt may remain in the carpet fibers when using this method; therefore industry professionals may recommend only using chemical dry cleaning on an intermittent basis, such as between shampooing or steam cleanings.

Even if you choose to employ only one method of carpet cleaning, there are no exact formulas to follow. Each material you service will require knowledge of how to pre-treat stains, best remove dirt, and which detergents work best. This information should be included in the manufacturer's instructions of the equipment you use.

What You Will Need

Though it is tempting, especially when starting out and finances are tight, to purchase common rotary brush machines, you should resist the urge. These machines, even those designed for commercial spaces, are available for consumers to rent but produce mediocre results at best. Instead, invest time in researching more current and advanced machines.

Depending on the services you will be providing, consider these questions when deciding what type of equipment best meets your business's needs:

✓ If your choice is to offer multiple services (carpet, drapery, upholstery), choose a multi-functional machine to save time, energy, and money in alternating machines and additional purchases.

✓ Know what accessories you will need to complete each job.

✓ Understand the limitations and allowances of the manufacturer's warranty that comes with each piece of equipment.

✓ Pay attention to requirements of service contracts and other support issues.

✓ Talk with the manufacturer or equipment representative to see what types of training is available.

Commercial Cleaning Services

Janitorial Services

Janitorial clients are in every commercial building around you. Even the smallest business, office, or retail establishment needs to be cleaned daily, so you have a pool of possible clients with whom to grow.

What It Is

While janitorial crews perform the same tasks as maid service crews, janitorial jobs are much larger in scope and area. Janitorial companies may establish themselves by cleaning small offices and move upwards as their staff, confidence, and reputation grow.

Businesses and offices are only the tip of the proverbial iceberg when seeking new clients for your janitorial services. Consider these possibilities as well: medical facilities (including doctor's offices, urgent care facilities, and outpatient centers), food service businesses (such as restaurants and coffee shops), and even warehouses — where restrooms, public areas, employee rooms, and offices need attention.

As the business owner, your time will be best spent performing managerial tasks while you send your crews on location to clean, but since janitorial services usually take place during evening and night hours, you may choose to do the office tasks during the day and visit your crew during their work shift.

What You Will Do

Janitorial cleaning involves basic cleaning of large areas with specialized services, based on location and type of business. Janitorial services may include:

- ✓ Dusting

- ✓ Vacuuming

- ✓ Trash removal

- ✓ Restroom, lunch room, and common area cleaning

- ✓ Administrative office cleaning

As you grow and expand, you can also offer customers:

- ✓ Floor stripping, waxing, and buffing services

- ✓ Window cleaning

- ✓ Carpet shampooing/cleaning

- ✓ Specialized floor care

Servicing some clients, for example medical offices, will require knowledge on how to prepare and deal with certain issues such as blood-borne pathogens and proper disposal of medical waste. Food service clients have health and occupational safety requirements, and some retail establishments may have other guidelines they expect you to follow. Clarify everything with the client prior to implementing your janitorial crew's necessary precautions for that environment.

What You Will Need

Initial janitorial supplies and equipment cost a little more than common maid service supplies because you will need to have more supplies on hand, but nothing exorbitant. Here is a list of basic products you will need on-hand to complete normal janitorial jobs satisfactorily:

- ✓ Soap/detergent

- ✓ All-purpose cleaning solution

- ✓ All-purpose cleansing powder

- ✓ Glass cleaner

- ✓ Pumice sticks

- ✓ Disinfectant

Necessary equipment for your crews includes:

- ✓ Upright vacuum

- ✓ Wet/dry vacuum

- ✓ Bucket(s)

- ✓ Cleaning carts

- ✓ Sponges

✓ Spray bottles

✓ Broom and dustpan

✓ Mops, mop bucket, and wringer

✓ Carpet cleaning machine

✓ Wheeled trash cans or trash can coasters

✓ Extension ladder

✓ Step ladder

✓ Squeegees

✓ Putty knife/floor scraper

✓ Three-pronged adapters

✓ Extension cords

✓ Dust cloths

✓ Floor signs, such as "wet floor" or "closed"

✓ Scrub pads

✓ Wax applicator

If you offer special services as you grow, you will need specific equipment for those jobs.

Miscellaneous Services

Whether you center your business on consumer cleaning, commercial services, or a combination of both, there are a variety of additional niche services you may want to consider offering, either independent of your cleaning business or as a component.

This section provides an overview of these services. Each requires different training and skills and may require specialized equipment. If you find one or more that interest you or that your customers request or have an interest in, you will need to research the area thoroughly before adding to your regular services.

Past cleaning-service owner and current owner of "The Cleaning Services Directory" Matt Goodwin, found that offering additional services for existing clients was a nice break from cleaning. "I would offer handyman or pet sitting services for clients when they went on vacation. I found that the clients were already comfortable with me in their home, so it was easier for them to hire me for other services than it would be for them to go find another company to provide those services. I did very well in that regard."

Disaster Cleaning/Restoration

Carpet cleaning and janitorial firms may be involved in disaster cleaning and restoration services, but this area requires a solid knowledge of the techniques and procedures involved before you launch into it. Knowledge of smoke, fire, and water damage is important.

Working with clients as a disaster cleaning and restoration service involves basic training. After your business is established, you will be able to work with contractors and insurance adjusters to provide these services. Training is available through the Restoration Industry Association. Additional information can be found in Appendix A.

Window and Blind Cleaning

On a smaller scale, maid and janitorial services may offer window and blind cleaning to their customers as part of standard services, but window and blind cleaning may be viewed as a specialty service within the industry.

Window cleaners may work outside on larger buildings and service the windows on the building — so if you do not mind heights, this might be a service to consider offering. You will need to clean both sides of the window regardless of weather. Pricing for window cleaning services begins at $1 to $3 per pane, or you may choose to charge per window. Other window cleaners charge by the job, basing their fees on a rate of $20 to $50 and up per hour. Cleaning windows is not simply removing dirt, but removing tape, glue, and paint from windows as well. Be sure you are aware of the depth of the cleaning job (if it is paint removal, test clean an inconspicuous spot to see how much time will be required) before quoting a price.

People routinely neglect cleaning their blinds until the buildup of dust and dirt is noticeable. But mini-blinds are not the only type of window covering you will be able to clean if you offer blind service to customers; consider also cleaning Venetian blinds, interior window shutters, Roman shades, vertical blinds, and pleated shades. Cleaning blinds is a labor-intensive process that requires special equipment to cut time and offer both a reasonable and profitable price to your customers. You will need to learn the process for removing and re-hanging blinds and training to use your equipment efficiently. In terms of business potential, the use of blinds outnumbers drapery by a margin of about 5 to 1, so this could be an area of growth for your business.

Ceiling and Wall Cleaning

Imagine all the pollutants in your air at home and in the office. If your ventilation system is not in prime condition or you live in a climate where you spend time indoors with the windows closed, those pollutants — everything from smoke, oil, nicotine, dust mites, and cooking grease, to name a few — have nowhere to go but your walls and ceilings.

Cleaning walls and ceilings can improve the health, cleanliness, and brightness of any commercial establishment or residence. Effective and cost-efficient compared to painting, thorough wall and ceiling cleaning can save building and home owners the time and cost of replacing walls and ceilings. Getting to know the types of walls you will encounter (such as porous, semi-porous, and non-porous finishes) and the proper cleaning methods for each to remove the filth and grime without damaging the appearance or finish of the wall or ceiling will take a bit of research. Vendors of wall and ceiling cleaning equipment should be able to provide training on the proper use of their equipment and accompanying chemicals.

4

Getting Off the Ground

Armed with the knowledge of the types of cleaning businesses and services you can choose from to establish your own business, you surely have creative ideas and possibilities in mind. Whether your decision comes down to residential services, a commercial cleaning business, or a mixture of the two, you need to know not only who your potential customers will be, but also what types of competition you will face in your area. You will also need to establish the business foundation to make your business dream a reality.

Which Cleaning Business Is For You?

Cleaning businesses may offer services to consumer and commercial clients rather than specializing in one area. A foundational knowledge of the market potential and competition of each area will prepare you to meet the needs of your clients before you give your first estimate.

Residential/Consumer

Customer Base and Market Potential

Mention "maid service" and people immediately get a stereotypical vision in their heads of an older woman wearing an apron, a frilly cap, and sporting a feather duster with the implication of the family hiring the maid being wealthy and living in a family mansion. The reality of today's maid and residential house cleaning services, however, is nothing like that.

Maid service is becoming popular among people from a variety of lifestyles: working couples with families, homes with two or more incomes, singles who want more time to themselves and less time spent on tasks they dislike, senior citizens with limited abilities or interest in daily maintenance around the house, and retirees who want to do other things. Clients may include a growing group of middle- to upper-income families with disposable income and limited downtime who are willing to pay for and see the value of maid service both from a financial as well as a time-savings point of view.

Residential services are not limited to homes but are also provided to small offices, rental properties, new homebuilders, and multi-unit residential spaces. From this pool of possible clients are millions of clients who have the means to procure your services.

Competition

The main source of maid service competition is primarily other residential and commercial service companies. Do not let this deter you from forming your own service, as maid services are only as reputable and popular as their attention to quality and detail at a fair price. You may offer the same service as another company in your area, but if your service speaks for itself in terms of a quality job, you may just sway customers of other residential cleaning companies toward you.

You might also find competition, especially in smaller commercial settings such as offices and retail properties, with the company's employed cleaning staff. Just because a company or office space has a cleaning staff already does not preclude you from offering your services. Companies may be adding additional cleaning services for which their staff is not trained, or they may be working on limited time constraints. With the advent of outsourcing, businesses are looking for outside service providers to do the work of their employees at a lower price. Contacting businesses as possible clients also serves as a free, inexpensive yet powerful networking tool. A company or office may not need to use your services right now, but another time they may need someone to call for a specific job or may be asked by a colleague for a referral for a cleaning service. Though you will not make every contact a client, you can make every contact a colleague to help extend your name and services in the community.

Finally, your most formidable competition will come from your clients themselves. Cleaning is a job that anyone can perform; whether they can complete the job satisfactorily is subject to debate, of course, and every client has their own standards of acceptable cleanliness. Providing the best cleaning service is fundamental to your success. Reminding customers of the value in both time saved and quality service is the best defense against losing a client who believes they can do a better job.

Commercial/Janitorial

Customer Base and Market Potential

When asked what line of work they want to pursue as adults, children rarely reply, "I want to own a commercial cleaning business!" There is little chance of glamour, fame, and international acclaim from cleaning businesses, offices, and retail establishments after the daily staff has left for the day, but what the job lacks in popular appeal it makes up for with potential profits.

The range and variety of services you offer will determine the type of commercial businesses you approach. If you lean toward basic services such as vacuuming, dusting, window cleaning, and trash removal, virtually any business is a possible customer. This includes offices, office buildings, restaurants, schools, medical offices, museums, warehouses, nursing homes, hospitals, manufacturing facilities, retail establishments, and just about any other business. Perhaps specializing in a certain area of cleaning is more appealing. Maybe you have a high concentration of medical facilities in your city, or you enjoy working with the food-service industry. You may want to pursue in-depth training to offer the highest level of cleaning service to particular establishments and work only with those types of businesses. You can make your own decision based on your preferences, abilities, and the types of businesses in your area.

Competition

As with residential services, the stiffest competition you will face is other janitorial services in your area, both large and small.

Competing with smaller janitorial services, such as mom-and-pop or family-based businesses, is an opportunity to put your best foot forward and make your company stand out from the rest. These cleaners do business as a way to make extra cash on the side and do not take the additional step of establishing themselves as a business. They may not be properly insured or bonded, which detracts from their image as a professional business. While their services may be inexpensive, they may also have minimal quality controls and assurances regarding the performance of their work. When you directly compete with these businesses, your attention to professional detail will cause clients to take note. Having a solid business structure, maintaining insurance, and keeping a keen eye for quality services will boost your image and credibility with potential clients.

If your main competitor is a nationally known janitorial franchise, their name recognition and marketing budgets can be intimidating. These companies may have the latest in cleaning and janitorial equipment, company transportation, and software systems, but they also have problems smaller companies do not.

Larger pools of employees mean higher rates of employee turnover. Hiring employees and making certain they have the proper paperwork, training, and on-the-job experience to perform at an optimal rate takes time and energy. Fewer employees equals less time training and more time cleaning. Employee loyalty to the company's vision also decreases as the company size increases, so keeping staffs small and manageable leads to more motivated workers. Bigger companies may be able to send larger crews to work sites to offer more services, but more employees does not necessarily translate into higher quality.

You may also find yourself in competition with in-house cleaning staff. Completing the job in a more cost-efficient manner may lead the company to reconsider your services or hire your crews to perform services in addition to the company's basic cleaning.

If you are serious about starting your own cleaning business, do not allow a little competition to chase you away. Realizing that someone has the same idea and offers similar services to yours should not deter you from pursuing your dream.

Before finalizing your choice for the type of business and cleaning services you want to offer, check the Yellow Pages or visit the Chamber of Commerce in your locale to survey existing cleaning businesses in your area. Note the contact information and give these businesses a call. You can talk with them as if you were a potential client or share with them your interest in pursuing a cleaning business and ask them questions. Find out what services they offer, what their charge for each, and other pertinent details. Do not waste their time, and keep your interaction strictly professional. There is no need to insult or aggravate the competition before you get your business going.

The beauty of the cleaning industry is that there is always a way to do something different or better. Knowing what you will face in your local market service area will give you insight on how to prepare your business to meet needs not already addressed by current companies. Do not fear competition; learn from it.

Legal Structure of Your Cleaning Business

Before you get ahead of yourself, determining the legal structure on which you will build your business is crucial. You need to know what type of ownership your business is before you can apply for a license. The availability of startup capital from lending institutions varies by type of business structure as well. A number of legal business structures exist, but for a cleaning business you will want to consider one of three types: sole proprietorships, partnerships, and corporations.

Sole Proprietorship

Cleaning companies, even those that go on to become corporations, commonly start as sole proprietorships. A sole proprietorship means you are the owner of the business and that you are doing it by yourself (though states may extend sole proprietorship status to spouses). You may employ others to perform cleaning duties and office tasks, but you have sole legal obligation for the company.

Sole proprietorships are best if your company makes less than $1 million in profit per year. As a sole proprietor, state and federal income tax laws consider you and your business as one entity for purposes of collecting taxes, and your business taxes will be paid via your personal income tax filing at the same rate. This may sound a little unnerving, but the profit your business makes equals your personal earnings. The more business you do, the higher your profits and the higher your tax rate; the difference is that as a business owner, you can take your business's itemized tax deductions on your personal income tax return. This will ensure that your profit and your business's bottom line will be lower than if you made the same amount of annual income from another employer.

Advantages of sole proprietorships include:

- ✓ Easier, less costly, and less time-consuming to establish than partnerships or corporations

- ✓ Decision-making power rests with you, saving time and energy

- ✓ Confidentiality — you have no obligation to publish any information about your company other than what you choose

- ✓ Ability to diversify, expand, change, or add services as you wish without meetings or other input

- ✓ Protection of personal assets from loss from a lawsuit or other legal action through liability insurance

Disadvantages of sole proprietorships include:

- ✓ Subject to "unlimited liability" — personal assets (home, real estate, and other personal belongings) can be seized for payment if your business fails or to fulfill other debts incurred by your business

✓   If you die, your business dies with you

✓   May be a limiting business form as your business expands

✓   Higher earnings equal higher tax bracket

✓   Lending institutions may be reluctant to offer financing options

✓   Not viewed as a "sophisticated" form of business the way partnerships and corporations may be

Partnership

Businesses jointly owned by two or more people (partners) are considered partnerships. All partners are equal in terms of profits and losses. Additionally, all partners are personally liable to the amount of invested equity in terms of lawsuits or losses. Each partner pays business income taxes based on the percentage of the business they own.

Forming a partnership can be a good financial idea for larger companies as each partner in the partnership represents a different source of funding. The more partners involved, the more money with which to establish your business. However, if a partner engages in or agrees to third-party contracts for any purpose, the partner signs the contract on behalf of the partnership, not as an individual.

One major drawback of partnerships is they are an unlimited liability type of investment — an investment where a partner or investor can lose an unlimited amount of money.

Other considerations for partnerships:

✓   More than one owner means more variety of skills and ideas with which to guide and grow your business.

✓   Startup capital increases as the number of partners grows.

✓   Lending institutions may look at partnerships as a better credit risk when seeking financing options.

✓   Entering into a partnership requires a high level of trust and confidence among the owners/partners.

✓   Personalities may clash if partners have differing ideas on which way the business should go.

✓   Businesses held as partnerships can be difficult to sell.

✓   Partnerships, while they may be started between friends and families with the best of intentions, occasionally lead to irreconcilable differences.

Corporations

Corporations differ from both partnerships and sole proprietorships for one simple reason: they are created as completely separate business entities from the individual owner. In cases of bankruptcy, personal assets are safe from seizure. Only business assets can be liquidated. If your business makes $1 million or more in profits per year, you may want to consider incorporation.

Establishing a business as a corporation can be done at the state or federal level, but is an expensive proposition. A larger investment is required than if you began as a partnership or sole proprietorship. Beginning entrepreneurs may be advised to starting out as a corporation because of this expense. It is, however, an option to remember as your business and services grow.

Other considerations for incorporation include:

✓   No one person can be held financially liable in a corporation.

✓   Raising capital for larger projects is easier.

✓   Death does not affect the operation of a corporation.

✓   There are tax advantages as a corporation.

✓   Other businesses may view corporations as a more sophisticated, serious business.

✓   You will need to hire a professional tax advisor to understand corporate tax breaks and get good tax planning advice.

✓   Preparation and publication of annual expenditure reports is required.

✓   Company information is available and open to the public.

✓   Going down from a corporation to a partnership or a sole proprietorship can be difficult while moving up to a corporation can be easier.

Lawyer/Legal Advisor

Regardless of which business structure you choose for your cleaning business, sometime you will need the advice of a qualified legal advisor or lawyer to answer specific questions affecting the operation of your business.

You may not need a lawyer at the onset of your venture, but it is a good idea to take the time to establish a positive relationship and retain the services of a lawyer early in your business venture. Then when the need arises, you will not have to spend all your time searching and interviewing candidates.

When you are seeking legal counsel, ask friends, family, and other acquaintances with business experience for referrals. Bankers regularly work with lawyers, so seek their advice. Clarify fees in advance, and get the fee structure in writing.

Every business equates time with money, and lawyers are no different. If you engage the services of your previously retained lawyer, keep your costs manageable by contacting the lawyer only when necessary. Prepare your questions in advance. Do not call to converse or discuss trivial matters. Be respectful of their time. Consult your lawyer for advice regarding:

- ✓ Contractual matters or disputes

- ✓ Establishing your business structure

- ✓ Leasing equipment

- ✓ Creating letters of intent

- ✓ Personnel or human resource issues

- ✓ Suits or pending litigation

- ✓ Debt collection process

- ✓ Review of contracts or legal documents prior to signing

In the process of interviewing potential lawyers for your business, pay close attention to:

- ✓ Their comfort level when interacting with you

✓   How well they understand your needs

✓   Their ability to communicate on a basic level rather than with a highly technical vocabulary

✓   Openness and friendliness

Make certain the lawyer you retain is someone you are comfortable working with. Consultation may be necessary for stressful reasons; limit the amount of stress you will encounter by hiring someone you work well with.

Questions you can ask potential lawyers are:

✓   What are your fees and billing terms/conditions?

✓   How soon after I contact you with a problem can your schedule accommodate me?

✓   What is your availability for my business?

✓   Are you familiar with the cleaning industry?

✓   What resources do you use to keep abreast of current industry procedures and issues?

✓   Do you have experience advising small business owners?

✓   What is your success rate in terms of tax problems or litigation?

✓   Do you offer informational meetings, workshops or seminars?

Accountant

If quality service and attention to detail is the heart of your business, then financial stability and fiscal management is the backbone.

Accountants are certified professionals who perform a variety of necessary tasks for the financial health of your business. In addition to preparing tax returns and other financial statements, accountants can also prepare your budgets, advise on expenditures, give tax advice, and set up a bookkeeping system for your daily operations. Trained and certified accountants can provide you with statistical data to guide your business decisions and help you see trends to capitalize on for maximum growth. They can provide advice for financial strategies and analyze past data to guide future actions.

The process of hiring an accountant is a bit similar to that of hiring a lawyer. Begin by seeking out the advice of friends and family with business backgrounds, bankers, and even referrals from a local chamber of commerce.

Accountants have a pool of clients with whom they work, so you will schedule times with the accountant that work with both of your schedules. Questions you will want to ask prospective accountants before hiring them include:

- ✓ Do you have experience doing the books for a small business?

- ✓ Do you have a basic hourly rate? If so, what services are included? If not, what are your fees for different services?

- ✓ What times are you available for consultation?

When first starting out, hiring the services of an accountant may seem to be an unnecessary expense, especially if you have basic bookkeeping or record-keeping experience. If you begin small, you may choose to do the financial bookkeeping yourself to get to know your company's spending limits, profit margins, earning percentages, and financial foundation. This is not a bad way to start, but unless you also possess the in-depth knowledge of tax law, hiring an accountant to get the tax breaks you are entitled to is a solid idea.

If you are interested in serving as your own bookkeeper early in the game and lack confidence or knowledge on basic bookkeeping standards, there is a wealth of material in bookstores and libraries to get you started. One option is *The Complete Guide to Working for Yourself: Everything The Self-Employed Need to Know About Taxes, Record Keeping and Other Laws* from Atlantic Publishing.

Choosing and Registering Your Business Name

Since choosing your type of business and collection of cleaning services you will offer clients, you might have had a handful of possible business names in mind. Though you may be tempted to skip this section, there are reasons why spending a little time on the creation of the name everyone will come to know as your business is so crucial.

Your business name:

- ✓ Needs to reflect the type of business you are running, as it will identify you as long as the business is yours and is in operation.

- ✓ Will be more than a name; it will be a marketing tool and will create an image to potential clients.

- ✓ Should be memorable and catchy.

- ✓ Should have broad customer appeal.

- ✓ Needs to be easy to spell.

✓ Will represent you as a cleaning business, so avoid the word "maid" in your name. Maid services may imply a range of services in addition to cleaning.

✓ Should avoid generic, sound-alike names (for example, Top Cleaning, Top Dog Cleaning, Top Hat Cleaning). You may lose business because a client thinks they are calling your service when they are not.

Steps in choosing and registering a business name

1. Make a list of four or five possible names you like. One suggestion is to use your last name in the business name. Unless you have a common name like Jones or Smith, it may be easier to remember a real name as opposed to a fictitious one.

2. Perform searches to make certain the name you want to use is not already in use. You will want to search at the local, state and even federal level if you have chosen to do business as a corporation. Places you can check for business names that already exist are:

   ✓ Yellow Pages

   ✓ County Clerks, who have a local deed registry

   ✓ Libraries, who may do name searches for a fee

   ✓ Newspaper classified advertisements

   ✓ Trade journals — magazines for the cleaning industry

3. After you determine your name is not being used at the local level, you can register it at the county level. While there may be a fee for this, registering at the county level is a smart move

to ensure no one else can legally register or use your company's name.

4. Business owners also can go on to register their name at the state level. You may be able to do the search portion yourself online by searching "secretary of state" and your state name into any search engine to find the correct site and the search process. You can also do this research at the secretary of state's office. You will need documented proof that your name is not in use before you can file for state registration. Following your payment of a registration fee and filling out the official paperwork, your business name will be yours to use.

5. The Department of Commerce in your state can help answer and/ or direct your questions to the proper registration agency.

If the name you have chosen is a fictitious one (meaning not the actual name of a person), you are required to file for a fictitious business name. The process may seem intimidating, but it is fairly inexpensive ($10-$50), easy (less than 30 minutes) and a requirement if you are doing business in any name other than your own. You can also just use your name as your business name, but you would only be able to use your name to represent your business. For example, if a cleaning business owner named Richie Frazee wanted to name his business after himself to avoid the necessity of filing, he would need to name the business "Richie Frazee." "Richie Frazee's Cleaning" would not be acceptable, as there is no such person named "Richie Frazee's Cleaning." It may be tempting to try this alternative, but consider how many people would see "Richie Frazee" and know it is a cleaning business.

There are other reasons to register your fictitious name:

✓   Your fictitious name is required to open a business bank account.

✓ It makes you more visible and attractive to potential clients.

✓ It keeps your name as yours. Just as you cannot use another registered business name, no one can use yours.

✓ This assumed name can open doors to vendors and retailers to give you discounts on products and equipment offered only to businesses.

✓ It establishes you as a legitimate business in your community.

✓ Your business has no legal standing without it. This means you have no ability to collect debts owed you, and there is no official record of your business.

Appendix B includes a worksheet to help guide you in creating a business name for your cleaning company.

Applying for a Business License

Every state, county, and city has different legal considerations for obtaining a business license. Specific information on the business licensing procedure in your area can be found by contacting your county clerk.

In establishing yourself as the owner of a business, you are required to comply with all federal, state, and local regulations. You must register your business to file tax documents. If you fail to obtain the necessary license and registration, you are not considered a legitimate business and cannot claim any federal or state tax opportunities afforded to businesses.

A business license only allows you to operate your business legally in a specified location or area. It does not refer to your having met any cleaning requirements or standards. Unlike other business owners, such as beauticians and electricians, there is no accrediting body for cleaners.

Commercial clients may ask if you have had training if you are performing a specialized or potentially hazardous service such as chemical removal, but no additional skills beyond common cleaning knowledge are required for your business.

Even sole proprietors need to obtain a business license. If you are working for a client and something you did deliberately or accidentally were to cause you to come under legal scrutiny, and you are not properly licensed, the lack of a business license can give the impression that you have done something wrong. It could imply that you are not a legitimate business, and you could be subject to large fines — large enough to wipe out your profits, your assets, and your business.

Licensing paperwork varies in length and breadth from one state to another, but is reasonably easy to complete. The important questions are about the type of business you are licensing and the area in which you plan to do business. The cost for sole proprietors is commonly less than $250 a year, which may seem high, but if you are serious about your business, it is a step you need to take.

Insurance and Bonding

If you are doing business as a sole proprietor, you may have the impression that only larger companies or corporations need to deal with insurance and bonding — and you would be dead wrong. All it takes is one client making a claim against you, your employees, or your service, and you may find yourself in the midst of an intense and expensive lawsuit. A business without insurance is a business just waiting for something to happen.

Liability insurance is a necessity. Because you will be entering homes and businesses, you open yourself to claims of theft, damage during cleaning, or even damage to the structure of the building. Damages from cleaning services may be accidental in nature. Perhaps your vacuum jars the leg of a coffee table causing a ceramic statue to topple. You could slip on a wet floor and reach for the countertop only to knock a glass to the tile. You may mistake a bottle of an abrasive cleaner and scratch the finish from a delicate item. In the winter, you may enter a client's home with mud on your shoe and unknowingly permanently stain a section of carpet. While it sounds ridiculous, you might cause water or fire damage to a home. Stranger things have happened, and if it has happened to another cleaner, it can happen to you.

Liability insurance is inexpensive, but it will help boost your credibility and professional image. Reverse roles and imagine an uninsured cleaner coming into your home. It's essential. You will want to include this insurance coverage information in the service handbook you share with customers so that they can verify with your insurance agent that you are properly insured.

You may be able to obtain liability insurance for your business by contacting the agent who already handles your homeowner's or car insurance to see if you can add the service. It is possible you could get a discount for multiple insurance accounts through one agent. Alternately, you can search for agents who offer small business liability insurance plans through the phone book or via the Internet.

Be sure to check over your policy to make sure it includes all the elements you want covered for your business. Common areas of coverage all cleaning business policies should include are:

- ✓ **General Aggregate Limit** — the maximum amount of losses a company will cover during a policy period.

- ✓ **Product/Completed Operations Limit** — a policy standard that does not necessarily apply to cleaners. It refers to coverage from lawsuits based on anything you might sell or give to your client.

✓ **Personal and Advertising Injury Limit** — which involves loss to another person or business based on libel, slander, defamation, the violation of right to privacy, theft of ideas, or infringement of copyright, trademark, title, or slogan as a result of your advertising. This is where you need to be careful to research competing companies to avoid using their logos, slogans, or trademarks in your business, as well as being professional and avoiding the urge to negatively comment on the business of another in touting your own.

✓ **Fire Damage and Medical Payments** — in case you unintentionally cause a fire or injure a client in the line of service.

✓ **Care, Custody, and Control** — a rarely used area of liability policies. Anything placed temporarily in your custody: a pet or plant a client asks you to watch while on vacation that dies is an example. You can eliminate worry about this if you inform clients that your services include cleaning only.

✓ **Key Loss** — in case you lose a client's keys. You can have a provision for it in your liability coverage; however, the best guard against needing the coverage is solid accountability and security standards by locking keys in a safe place when they are not in use.

If you employ independent contractors to add services to your business, you will need to purchase liability insurance for each person with whom you contract. This will change your policy and increase your rates, but is important. Check with your agent on the proper procedure.

Bonding is protection against theft. Bonding is inexpensive and valid for one year at a time. It covers litigation costs as well as the value of the stolen item (up to the amount of the bond purchase price) if you are convicted of the crime. Conviction requires significant incriminating evidence or a reliable witness, so even if a client claims you or your employees stole, it will require solid proof and not just circumstantial evidence.

Even if you do not use your surety insurance bonds, the peace of mind and professionalism having such a bond provides boosts your reputation among potential clients. Ask your insurance agent about surety (also referred to as dishonesty) bonds. If they cannot provide them to you, ask for a referral to someone who can. You will need to purchase a surety bond for each employee you hire. Keep your insurance and bonding policies up to date; nothing is worse than thinking you have insurance coverage and finding out that your coverage has lapsed or become outdated.

Developing Your Business Plan

Think for a moment about the last time you went on a vacation or trip away from home to an unfamiliar location. Did you arrive on time as expected? Or did you spend time trying to find your way, getting haphazard instructions, or guessing about where you might end up only to find out you had miscalculated your location?

Mapping out the steps and directions to an unfamiliar but exciting destination before you get started is no different than creating a business plan for your cleaning company. No doubt you are full of energy and ideas for your new business, but you need to face the journey of building your business with the proper tools, guidelines, and plans.

Why You Need A Business Plan

Like the scenario mentioned above, embarking on a trip or a business venture without a solidly planned, thorough vision of where you are going, everything you will need, and how you will arrive at your destination is an invitation for trouble or even disaster. Without a map or a structured analysis of the journey, you will waste time, money, and energy. You will spend more time solving problems than enjoying yourself.

The time invested in creating your detailed business plan will pay off in a multitude of ways. Most notably, funding sources will rarely offer startup capital to a business with no structure or plan of operation. Since you will have to sit and think through every element of your business, you will have the chance to examine your ideas for potential weaknesses and problems before you start and prior to investing money or time into something that might not go as smoothly as you anticipated. Looking over your business plan will give you a footing in the reality of your business. Even though you know you want to own your own cleaning business, you may not have thought through every detail, and working on your business plan can help you clarify goals you are still fuzzy about. A good business plan will show you what you need — in terms of facilities, staff, equipment, capital, and marketing — to succeed from the moment you start to five or more years down the road. Furthermore, a well-organized business plan can be a valuable and reassuring reference guide to consult when your business gets stressful.

Suggestions on Completing Your Business Plan

Although the components of the business plan are presented here in a particular order, you may not complete your plan in this order. For example, one of the foundational parts of your business plan is the table of contents, but you may find it easier to do a rough draft outline of the business plan, fill in the components of that plan as you acquire the necessary information and research, and then come back to the table of contents and refine it after the plan is compiled. You may also choose to work on the sections you already have data on and then move to more involved portions. Or you may want to work through the entire plan at once finishing a rough draft, and then go back and supplement each section with research in a revision process.

If you are planning to keep your business operational for any length of time, you are going to spend a large amount of time with your business, so resist the urge to rush through your business plan. Give your plan the same respect and time you will be paying to your daily business operations. Things will run much smoother with this kind of forethought. Your business is worth it.

Before you enact your plan, share it with trusted, respected, knowledgeable business colleagues. Nothing — not even the best or most recent data — is as valuable as having your plan filtered through the eyes of someone who has been in your shoes. Put their expertise to good use to help you achieve success.

Components of Your Business Plan

Your business plan will be unique to your business and the services you will offer your clients. However, the basic structure of your plan will need to incorporate the following elements to be sure you include all the necessary details for yourself as well as potential investors and lenders.

A standard business plan includes:

Section 1
- Introduction
  Your business plan will start with:
  - A cover page
  - Table of contents
  - Vision statement or statement of purpose

Section 2

- Business Summary

     The heart of your business plan is an in-depth presentation of the necessary elements of running your business and how you will achieve them:

  - Company Mission Statement
  - Company Goals
  - Company Operations
  - Inventory
  - Start-up Timetable
  - Organizational Plan, including:
    - Management structure
    - Staffing needs and procedure
    - Professional consultants and advisors
    - Legal structure
    - Licensing and permits
  - Marketing Strategy, including:
    - Description of the ideal customer and market
    - Business location analysis
    - Competition analysis
    - Promotional and Marketing Plan
  - Financial Plan, including:
    - Current information
      - Startup funding sources
      - Location needs: Fixtures, furniture, and supplies
      - Equipment needs
      - Insurance and bonding
      - Sample statements such as:
        - Balance sheet
        - Profit and Loss statement
        - Personal financial statements
        - Personal federal income tax returns

- Break even analysis
- Projected information:
  - Projected income for about three years
  - Projected cash flow statements for about three years
  - Potential worst-case income and cash flow statements in case your plans do not meet projections

Section 3
- Conclusion

  Now that you have presented your plan's details, you will need to wrap up your ideas.
  - Summary of the important points of your plan
  - Appendices of important documents such as market research studies, sample advertisements, lease/rental information, licensing documents, and others.

Following is an in-depth look at these three sections and what you will need to finish each part of your plan.

Section 1: Introduction

A cover page

A simple cover page reflects your professionalism.

Table of contents

You may want to wait to compile your table of contents or may choose to work from the outline presented here. Be sure every section of your business plan is represented in your business plan.

Vision statement or statement of purpose

In the creation of your business you will create both a vision and mission statement. While it may be confusing at first, a vision statement is a snapshot of what you hope your company will become, and a mission statement is how your company will accomplish that vision.

A vision statement is a short — a few sentences tops — first-person statement of what you want your company to achieve:

- ✓ The Patricia Carter Cleaning Company is the premier maid service in Central Ohio.

- ✓ XYZ Janitorial Service believes every office deserves a through daily cleaning.

Section 2: Business Summary

Company Mission Statement

A mission statement takes the umbrella of your vision statement and presents it in terms of how you will achieve that vision. Mission statements are written to inspire and guide employees on a daily basis, and they can be used in marketing and shared with customers.

Sample mission statements:

- ✓ PM's Cleaning and More provides customer satisfaction, attention to detail, and quality work at a quality price.

- ✓ Comet Carpet Cleaners strives to bring each customer the best cleaning service possible through trained employees using the latest techniques in the service industry.

For more help in designing your own vision and mission statements, see the worksheets Creating Your Vision Statement and Creating Your Mission Statement in Appendix B.

Startup Timetable

From the planning stage to the point where you open your doors for business, your startup timetable is your guide to what tasks you need to accomplish, the contacts you need to make, and the fundamental plans that have to be in place before you can service your first client. In addition to completing your business plan, you need to make appointments, apply for licenses, consult with insurance agents, determine how to hire and train staff, and choose marketing strategies to reach clients, among others.

Organizational Plan, including:

Management structure. If you are a sole proprietor, your management structure will start with you and work down through your advisors and consultants to your administrative staff, should you choose to include them in your business, then down to your crew supervisors and cleaning staff.

Partnerships, on the other hand, begin with all the partners at the top of the organization, moving on to advisors, consultants, and administration, and then to crew supervisors and cleaning staff.

Corporate management structures vary. After looking at structures of other corporations, consult with your advisors and choose a plan that works best for your business.

Staffing needs and procedure. The questions you will want to answer regarding staffing your business include knowing the number of employees you will need to get started and maintain your business. You will also need to address how you will recruit, interview, and train your employees, employee expectations and performance reviews, raises, and termination procedures.

Professional consultants and advisors. Even if you have not hired a lawyer and/or accountant yet, or you plan to do all the business tasks yourself, use this section to list those individuals with whom you plan to consult and ask for advice. Not only will this be a reference for you to consult when the time and need arise, but potential investors will view your willingness to seek advice as an asset.

Legal structure. Describe here the business format you selected: sole proprietorship, partnership, or corporation.

Licensing and permits. Without a business license you are not considered a professional business, and you are opening yourself for a host of problems in the future. Include information here about the licenses or permits you plan to obtain. If you have applied for licenses and/or permits but have yet to receive confirmation on them, list those details here and update this section as things change.

Marketing Strategy, including:

Description of the ideal customer and market — Describe your ideal customer(s). Are you offering services as a residential cleaning service, a commercial service provider, or a combination of both? What market area are you drawing from? How many potential customers can you realistically target as needing your services?

Business location analysis — What are the positive and negative attributes of the location you have chosen as your main office/business location? Think about traffic patterns, the neighborhood itself, adjacent businesses, or buildings.

Competition analysis — In your area as well as within your type of service group, who are your competitors? Do they offer more service? Better service? Lower prices? More options? Are they meeting the needs of the customers in your market or are there gaps in services where your company might be able to take advantage?

You also need to understand not only who your competitors are but also why your prospective customers might choose their services over you. What sets your business apart from them? How are you different?

Promotional and Marketing Plan — After detailing your customer profile and competition analysis, you need to think through your plans on how to promote and market your business to those customers to build your business.

Through your competition analysis, you have determined how to differentiate yourself from the variety of services available. Now think about how you will reach customers. Will you rely on newspaper and phone book advertisements? Posting on free bulletin boards in local businesses? Phone calls to potential clients? Cleaning businesses, both commercial and consumer, have also developed a presence on the Internet by publishing web pages promoting their business services, fees and contact information.

There is no guarantee the advertising money you spend will lead directly to the clients you want. Test the promotional business a little at a time to see how your efforts are received. If your marketing has positive results, think of ways to enhance it. If not, head back to the drawing board and refine your strategies. The beauty of the business plan is that nothing is written in stone. You can tweak the elements until they are a reflection of the business you want to represent.

Financial Plan, including:

Current information:

Startup funding sources — Where will your startup money come from? Who will you approached as potential financiers, investors, or partners in your business, and how much do you estimate they will provide? Banks, lending institutions, and individuals can be mentioned here.

Location needs: Fixtures, furniture, utilities, and office supplies — Finding the perfect location, even if you work from your home, is only half the battle when establishing your business. All the things you need for daily operations cost money, and they should be examined with a critical eye to ensure they are necessary before you spend your startup capital on them.

Fixtures and furniture do not need to be elaborate or expensive, just functional. If you work from a home office, you may already have these items in place. Utilities, such as gas, electric, water, and phone service, are necessities. With a home office, you can estimate these on a per-month basis, and you may be able to deduct the cost of them on your income taxes. (For more information, see "Taxes" in Chapter 5.)

Equipment and Cleaning Supplies — Regardless of the services you plan to provide customers, you will need to purchase equipment to supplement what you already own. You may also be able to rent or lease the equipment. How often will you use the equipment? Do you have a place to store it between uses if it is not something your crews will use on a daily basis?

While you may already have all the cleaning supplies you need to start your business, you will need to keep your cabinets stocked to assure you have enough to complete every job in a timely manner. What solutions and supplies will you use most? How much do you anticipate spending weekly? Monthly? Can you buy concentrations in bulk and mix the solutions yourself? Or will you use customer products to cut down on your supplies investment?

Insurance and bonding — The information you will need here can come directly from your insurance statements or estimates from your insurance agent.

Sample statements —

- ✓ Balance sheet

- ✓ Profit and Loss statement

- ✓ Personal financial statements

- ✓ Personal federal income tax returns

- ✓ Break even analysis

Projected information — In establishing your business, you have to forecast your sales and expenses to know where you are headed. At the start of your business it is a difficult task to anticipate where your profits and losses will be, but you need to project to the best of your ability.

Forecasting serves two main objectives: learn where your costs come from and anticipate what you will earn. Understanding your risks in relation to your profit potential will help give you a more realistic idea of where your profits will actually fall.

Projected cash flow statements for one year — Projecting your cash flow is using your knowledge to make an educated guess about how much your business can reasonably make in a set period. Cash flow is not about the profits you hope to earn; it is the up-and-down pattern of profits versus costs. Seek the advice of your accountant for more details. They have experience projecting and have insight into the specifics you will need to consider.

Potential worst-case income and cash flow statements should your plans do not meet projections. — Having a backup plan is crucial. Take the time now to develop your strategies with trusted colleagues and consultants so if the need for these plans arises, you are confident they were thoroughly thought through under less stressful circumstances. For help in estimating your cash flow, visit the Quarterly Cash Flow worksheet in Appendix B.

Case Study: Rick Crow

Partners In Grime House Cleaning

Kansas City, MO

www.partnersingrime.com

Rick Crow, President

If you are looking to get into the cleaning business because it seems like an easy way to make money and be your own boss, rethink your strategy before you sign your first client.

Unless you have the necessary skill set to run a business, creating a thriving cleaning company will be difficult. Even the best cleaner in the world cannot build a successful company unless he or she is good with the business aspect of running a cleaning business. Employee management, client development, customer service and research all go into the mix. Even though cleaning is a job, knowing how to clean or being the best cleaner in the world is the least important skill in starting a business. Anyone may be able to clean a home to an acceptable level, but not everyone can manage employees, market/sell your services, and provide outstanding customer service.

Contemplate how you want your business to look. Are you just trying to clean a few homes and create a job for yourself, or do you want to build an actual business? Although these sound similar, they are two different ventures. If you want income from cleaning houses, you can do this relatively easily and cheaply. However, if you want to start a professional residential cleaning business, anticipate needing $50,000 to $100,000 in working capital. With this initial investment you may expect to reach profitability in one or two years. The money will be used for extensive marketing and initial support staff. If you determine your best opportunity for success is to run a cleaning business rather than having a cleaning job, run your business as a business owner from the start. Beginning as a cleaner and trying to work your way back into the office/managerial position is difficult.

Case Study: Rick Crow

The best part of owning a cleaning business is the freedom it affords you as your own boss. Being able to spend more time with your family than you can with other businesses is a positive aspect. Starting with solid goals and following through with hard work is the way to succeed.

5

Developing Your Financial Plan

When it comes to starting your own small business, it is impossible to over-plan. For every problem that could happen you need to have a solution at least in mind, if not already on paper, and nothing presents more obstacles for entrepreneurs than money issues.

Money matters are not an entertaining element of planning your business, but they are the crucial. No money coming in means no business going out.

In addition, the more thoroughly developed and researched your financial plan, the more likely you will be able to convince others to help you get started — in the form of loans or other startup funds. Take advantage of your planning time to strategize your budget down to the smallest detail. It will pay off in the end.

Evaluating Costs for Startup & Operations

At the start of your business, calculating your expenses and income is an intimidating job that you have to do. It seems impossible to know how much you will earn and how much you will need to spend to continue operating when you have no financial history on which to base your calculations.

The bad news is you must do this in order to get off the ground. The good news is there is a wealth of tools to get you going.

Your financial planning revolves around two fundamental principles: what you expect your operating costs to be, and how much you can realistically expect to earn. Based on these figures, you can make an educated estimate of profits. You will be able to get a true feel for the profit potential of your business, what risks you will face, how much your startup costs will be and how long they will last. You will also be able to give investors an idea of what to expect from their contributions.

Startup Funds

Personal funds are a popular source of startup money, but they are not the only source. The key to the success of using your startup funds to keep your business humming is intelligent reinvesting in the business and structured, disciplined saving.

Startup capital can come from a variety of places. Your goal should be to have enough startup capital collected to cover your first year of expenses. Banks may not be a primary source of these funds, so disciplining yourself to save the money you will need is important. Potential sources of startup funds include yourself, partners, friends, family, acquaintances, banks, and government.

Yourself

Take inventory of your assets to see how much you have to begin with. This includes real estate equity, savings accounts, recreational equipment, collections with a market value, even automobiles. Also consider retirement accounts, investment holdings, and lines of credit. If you have an excellent credit rating, use that to your advantage. There is nothing wrong with beginning your business with credit cards if you are a responsible consumer and are aware of all the terms and conditions of your credit accounts.

Partners

You do not necessarily need a partner who wants to do the cleaning work with you. Perhaps someone you know or network with has the money to invest and is looking for a small business investment. Or you may find another person interested in cleaning with you or who has a niche in mind and is looking to partner with someone. Before joining services and funds, create a written agreement for your partnership with clear definitions of the expectations and responsibilities of each partner.

Friends, Family and Acquaintances

Cleaning business owners may have well-intentioned family and friends willing to loan them startup cash (consult your cash flow forecast in the next section to see when you can realistically expect to pay them back, if this is part of your agreement), be careful and aware of the issues that can crop up when personal relationships and money mix. If you are loaned money, put the agreement in writing. Conduct yourself professionally when discussing your business and the money, and be responsible enough to accept money only from those you know can truly afford it. Weigh the value of your relationship against the value of your business when determining whether it is worth it.

Banks

Here is where the time you spend researching and detailing your business plan can pay off. Banks and other lending institutions want to see proof that you have carefully considered all the elements that go into the creation of a successful business to know you are serious about your venture. Banks do not lend lightly, and they require collateral as a guarantee on their investment. Banks also help businesses establish themselves through means other than money. For example, they may offer resources and advice on startup, investing, money management systems, and other services.

Government

The Small Business Administration (SBA) has a wealth of information for small businesses that can answer your questions and help you locate funding sources and lenders. The easiest way to see how they can help is to visit their Web site at **www.sba.gov**. Depending on your niche or if you have a special background (women, veterans, minorities), there are additional funding options to help you get started.

Projecting Your Cash Flow

Your cash flow projection is not complicated. At the basic level it shows the variation between how much you earn versus how much you spend on a regular basis. Cash flow projections are a guard against finding yourself without money in the future, as you can plan for times when your projected income is less than your expenses.

Although your cash flow projection shows income and expenses for a short period, you should initially do the figures for the first year. Included in Appendix B is a worksheet for calculating your first 12 months of business. It is also a good idea to then do a quarterly review and update to keep a handle on what is coming your way.

When estimating your cash flow, note there are a number of expenses you will incur only once at the start of your business. Consider keeping salaries low for the first month as you get your business established and train your employees. Operating expenses will probably be low as well, and you can opt to pay a portion of your initial bills in the second or third month of operation without penalty. It is wise to spend as little of your startup money as possible until you have regular income from clients.

Break-even Point

The break-even point is defined what your business needs to make in profits each month to cover your expenses. This will guide you toward knowing how many jobs you will need to finish to bring in the money your business requires.

The break-even point is easiest to calculate by taking your anticipated monthly expenses and multiplying it by ten to arrive at a workable figure. This is an industry standard, and it should create a reasonable goal for you to meet in order to break even with costs and make a profit within the first two or three months of your business. It will give you insight into pricing your services to compete with other local businesses, and you can present it to business associates to get input on the feasibility of your numbers.

Revising Your Plans

Even solid cash flow forecasting will need to be revisited after your business is up and running. Dedicating time on a monthly basis to this task is a good idea, as it gives you a chance to see both successes and potential problems.

Since the cash flow is based on hypothetical numbers, compare this against real figures after you are established. How close were your calculations? What outside influences affected your ability to meet your goals? How does your workload and client demand vary by month, season, or type of optional services you provide? The cleaning business fluctuates and is rarely the same two months in a row. Consider how customers and their needs will change over the course of the year and plan to offer what they might need to ensure your continued growth.

Record Keeping for Success

With all the forms, forecasts, and plans necessary to the success of your business, having a solid record and bookkeeping system from the start is critical.

The first step should be to open a business account at your local bank. Transactions should only be for your business from this account — keep a separate account for your personal finances. When you open the account, you should order business checks and deposit slips. Speak with a bank representative and request that your monthly statements be cut off on the final day of each month. This makes reconciling your statements easier.

You must reconcile your account against your statement each month. Do this on time to save yourself unnecessary problems and to get a handle on any mistakes early. Your accountant can guide you in setting up a reconciliation system to help make tax preparation more expedient in the upcoming year.

Accounting Methods

Consider how you plan to record your financial transactions: cash system or accrual system. The choice is yours, but after you make the choice be consistent in your use of it to simplify managing your business books.

The cash system is similar to your checkbook system: When you receive a payment, you record the payment ,and when you pay an expense or bill, you record the expense on the day you pay it.

If you send a bill to a client at the end of March and they do not pay until April 12, the payment is recorded in your system as being paid on April 12, not the March billing date. The cash system is fairly simple, but it requires a little thought in that expenses are not recorded until they are paid. For example, if you receive vendor supplies or purchase equipment, the expense is not entered on the day you purchase but rather the day when you pay your invoice or bill.

The accrual system differs in that payments received and expenses incurred are recorded on the actual day when the transaction takes place. Bill the same client on March 25, and when you receive her payment on April 12, record the payment as being received on March 25.

While the cash system is easy because there is less to remember, consult your accountant or tax advisor for their recommendations. There are certain scenarios that work better with cash and others that fit with the accrual method.

Billing, Income, and Expense Records

How you bill clients and how you expect them to pay is as important to consider as how you will pay your own bills. These tasks can be set up with basic forms and will require minimum time to set up. As your business expands you may revisit these systems, but after you are comfortable with a particular system you will be able to rely on it over the course of your business's existence.

Billing Records

If you begin your business as a sole proprietor who does all the cleaning and arranges payment with each client on an individual basis, you still need a system of collections for reference purposes. You can tailor your billing system to meet your specific needs. Here are relevant questions to help you get started. If a client pays you after each cleaning session:

- ✓ Where do they leave the money?

- ✓ How do you acknowledge their payment?

- ✓ Do you accept cash, checks, or credit cards?

✓   What is your policy if they fail to leave payment or forget to pay?

✓   Who is responsible (if you have cleaning crews rather than servicing the job yourself) for getting the payment to you?

✓   How can you help the client pay for services in a timelier manner? (up front or monthly payments).

Extending credit to customers may be a necessary way to do business, especially with larger jobs or janitorial companies that service corporate accounts. Think through these possibilities when creating your billing system:

✓   Is there a way to align your billing system with the client's payment system?

✓   Do clients pay on specific days of the month?

✓   How can you ensure you receive their payment in a manner that benefits your business?

✓   Do they require a detailed invoice, a summary of services, or an itemized checklist?

✓   What are the penalties for late payment?

✓   Do you offer a discount for accounts paid within a certain frame of time, say 10 to 14 days after billing?

Income Records

Using either the cash or accrual system, create a simple chart (a sample Income Worksheet can be found in Appendix B) for recording income. If your crew supervisors are responsible for collecting, have them document the information on a daily basis and get the payments to you daily as well. They can take this sheet to their job site and leave it in your office safe on return.

If you bill clients, use the same form and documentation procedure to record payments as you receive them. Keep these records in a secure place for safety and easy reference.

Expense Records

Direct expenses are common expenses you will encounter in running your company. Supplies, equipment, advertising, and anything else you need in terms of materials to help keep your business running are a direct expense. Documentation (receipts, credit card statements, invoices, bills, and cancelled checks) is necessary to prove the importance of the expense to your business's operations and may be required by your accountant in preparing your taxes, so have a common collection procedure and storage spot for these.

Record these expenses as they occur or on a weekly or monthly basis. The sample Bi-Annual Expense Sheet in Appendix B shows what you will want to record. You can do this on paper, but if you set up a computer spreadsheet, you can configure the program to do the mathematical calculations for you.

Indirect expenses are the expenses of operating your business. If you work from home, a portion of your household expenses for such things as utilities, insurance, rent, or mortgage can be deducted from your taxable income. Chapter 10 has more information on indirect expenses and what qualifies as such. Your accountant will also have advice and insight on the current deductions for your business situation.

Capital expenses are the expenses of big-budget items such as expensive equipment or computer systems. Instead of deducting capital expenses in one lump sum, you will want to calculate depreciation — a percentage of the cost based on an average year's worth of use. Again, consult your tax advisor on depreciation policies and formulas and how to figure them into your overall expense reports.

Financial Considerations

Though method of payment is a simple issue, there are things you need to take into account when deciding what and how you will accept payment for your services.

Cash

The beauty of the cleaning business, especially in respect to residential cleaning, is that it is a cash business. You can set up an arrangement with clients so that payment is received immediately following service. Your clients will know the cost of the jobs you will be completing for them, so having the client leave cash or a check at the residence for you is a good practice. Be sure to leave a receipt with customers both to verify they paid you and that you have a record of it.

Checks

People occasionally may have insufficient funds to cover a check they have written. Determine in advance the penalties for returned checks (either a flat fee you will charge them or a percentage of the total) and stick to it. If returned checks become a problem with certain clients, you may want to require them to pay in cash or in advance. You are in a business to earn money, and if your services are something clients cannot afford, it is better to break the contract than risk your profits.

Credit Cards

Accepting credit cards for payment used to be a difficult and expensive process, but things have changed for the better. If you are uncertain about accepting credit cards for payment, do the research you need to do to get comfortable with it. Credit card acceptance is one easy way to expand your company's appeal to new clients. In addition, clients may have changed from writing checks to using debit cards, and you want your payment system to reflect the needs of your clientele.

Businesses may prefer to be billed for services, or they may prefer to track spending through use of a credit card. They may be more likely to add on services with a credit card than with cash.

Begin at your bank and inquire about a credit card merchant account. You may even find professional organizations with which you are currently affiliated who offer such services. With the growth of small businesses, merchant account providers are becoming competitive with their rates and services and may even include incentives for your business.

Each credit card account requires a separate application, fees, and verification procedure; thoroughly research these terms before agreeing to any conditions. Credit card companies routinely have transaction fees and expectations of you as a business associate, so know these as well.

One low-cost way to accept credit card payments is using **www.PayPal. com**. To use PayPal® you set up a business account and inform your clients that they can use their credit cards to pay you or can configure their PayPal® account to pay you directly from their banking institution.

While clients may occasionally not be comfortable using PayPal®, it is worth investigating to add to your list of payment options. It is free for clients to send you money, but PayPal® does take a small percentage of the money you receive as a fee. The immediate payment and lack of a required contract with credit card companies, though, may be worth it for your business.

Taxes

Taxes for the self-employed business owner require additional time and effort compared to simply recording tax information as an employee for someone else. The solid advice of a qualified accountant is essential to understand when and what to pay, what you can and cannot deduct, and what basic tax information you need to be successful and legally compliant. The following section provides you with important tax-related details you need to know, but it is also a good idea to consult with a local expert to make sure all your bases are covered.

When and What to Pay

Rather than an annual income tax, you will be expected to pay quarterly taxes on your business. The state and federal government will be looking for a payment covering estimated taxes for that period, and at the end of each year, you will reconcile your actual income with the amount of your estimated payments. If you overpay, you will get a refund, but if you have underpaid, you will be expected to make up the difference. Being as close to your actual income as possible is a good idea.

It is your responsibility to remember to make quarterly payments. The government does not invoice or bill you. If you think you can hold off or that taxes do not apply to you because you are not yet showing a profit, think again. The amount of money you may have to pay in penalties could wipe out any profits you have made, so do not risk your business by challenging the rules.

Deductions

The IRS requires any business deduction taken for a home-based business be the result of using a portion of your home regularly and exclusively for business. In this area, only business-related activities may be conducted: no spare bedroom where your family stores decorations or the kids play. If any machines or equipment are kept here, such as computers or telephones, they must be used only for conducting business.

This area must be used on a regular basis and as a principal place of business. If your home office does not qualify as your principal place of business (for example, you have another office and occasionally do business from your home), you may have other ways to deduct office expenses. You may also have a garage or separate structure that qualifies for deductions if you use it exclusively and regularly for business, such as repairing equipment or meeting clients.

Discuss this in-depth with your accountant before claiming any home-based deductions. Claiming a portion of your home as a business entity will require specific records, statements, and calculations you will need to use for verification purposes should you be questioned or audited. Be safe, not sorry, and enlist the help of a tax specialist to answer your questions.

6

Organizing Your Business

Moving into a space dedicated to serving as the home base for your cleaning business, whether in your home or a commercial location, brings another level of excitement to the entrepreneurship process. There are a variety of options to choose from when selecting your space, outfitting your business with office supplies, furniture and furnishings, and planning how to store equipment and inventory.

Choosing a Location

Before you get set up, you will want to spend time thinking about the benefits and drawbacks to establishing the location you will be using as your official place of business for your cleaning service: a home-based office or a leased/purchased space in a commercial or business area of town.

Whether a home-based office is more appealing or you like the prospect of commercial space, security and safety are important wherever you begin. It is essential that your office/building is secure and has a door that locks. As a company providing cleaning services when clients may not be home, you will be responsible for having a keys to their residence. You will also have maps, directions, and sensitive information about their homes, such as floor plans that you will need to share with your cleaning crews to properly complete your cleaning jobs. Keep these documents in a safe place where qualified employees can access them easily, but enforce security procedures. Think about what safe storage areas you will need for locking up keys. Even an experienced, outstanding staff will have turnover, and the safety of your client information and premises is an important responsibility.

From client accounts to vendor purchase orders to tax returns and legal papers, you will need a space where you can keep all your important records. Locked, two or three drawer metal filing cabinets should be adequate in the initial stage of your business.

You will also want to be near or have reasonable access to industrial or large capacity laundry facilities. Whether your cleaning services center on janitorial or residential customers, cleaning cloths, dust mop heads, and other materials will need regular washing and drying between jobs. There is the option of heading to the local coin laundry at the start of your business, but that takes time away from your office tasks.

Home-Based Business

For small companies just starting out, working from a designated area in your home is not only cost-effective and efficient, it is a practical solution. Working from home is a positive choice in several ways, but it offers a special set of challenges not found when renting or purchasing outside business space.

Benefits

An attractive reason for establishing your cleaning business office in your home is the number of tax incentives it provides. To deduct expenses for business use of your home, you must use part of your home in the following ways:

✓ Exclusively and regularly as your principal place of business

✓ Exclusively and regularly as a place where you meet or deal with clients or customers in the normal course of your trade or business

✓ In the case of a separate structure not attached to your home, in connection with your business

✓ On a regular basis for storage use

You must use a portion of your home only for your business. It must be a separate space or room, but it does not need to be permanently partitioned.

If you meet these guidelines, it is possible to deduct two types of business expenses from your taxes: direct expenses, the expenses that benefit only the business portion of your home, and indirect expenses, the expenses that apply in their entirety to your home as a whole.

Direct expenses apply to anything done to the part of you home officially and exclusively related to your business. These expenses are 100 percent deductible from your taxes. Expenses such as office furniture and equipment as well as services to your office only, such as painting and re-carpeting are direct expenses.

On the other hand, indirect expenses are expenses you incur with running your entire home. You will report 100 percent of these on your tax return and apply the percentage of business use of your home to determine the portion of these expenses that apply to your business. Examples of indirect expenses are your utilities (including gas, water, electric, sewer, trash collection), real estate taxes, deductible mortgage interest, casualty loss, rent, insurance, security systems, and depreciation.

Drawbacks

While working from a home office is sensible and a low-cost office space where businesses may remain for the duration of their business, there are legal considerations to account for before establishing your cleaning service from your home.

Communities may have laws and ordinances that limit and regulate commercial activities in residential areas. There may be laws regarding traffic patterns of potential clients coming into and parking in the neighborhood. Others may have no objection to the establishment of your business but impose restrictions on items like commercially marked vehicles (your cleaning crews' and your vendors'), signs, the coming and going of employees, and noise.

There are industry professionals who say beginning your business from home rather than a commercial setting makes the image you project to potential clients a less professional one, which will limit your success. Rather than eliminate an option based on what another person thinks, however, take time to think through the needs and potential of your business before making a final choice.

Considerations

Before applying for your business license, investigate which local ordinances govern small business in residential setting if you are planning to do work from your home. You may need to make changes, adjustments, or alterations to be legally compliant.

If you decide that working from a home office is the right choice for your business, be a considerate and conscientious neighbor. Keep noise and traffic to a minimum, especially when more of your neighbors are home. Remain professional and courteous if any of your neighbors complain; acknowledge the problem and tell them you will work toward an acceptable solution. Everyone around you is a potential client; treat them as such. You never know when they may need a cleaning service for their home or place of work.

Leased/Purchased Commercial Space

Not all homes have space for a home office; perhaps you have small children running around who make quiet moments almost non-existent. There may be available office space in a part of town with more potential clients, or you may feel the need to start your business in a new, fresh space full of potential. Whatever the reason leading you toward leasing or renting, your goal should be to find a functional, affordable space that meets the specific needs of your company.

Benefits

If you live in a competitive area of the city, your business may appear more credible and legitimate if you do business from a commercial space. However, new clients understand you are starting out small; they will judge you based on the quality of the jobs you complete for them.

A larger work space can have an added bonus of building camaraderie among you and your employees and your employees and each other. With the exception of your office staff, your crews will spend nearly all their working hours on location. They may come to your office in the morning to gather assignments or finish plans, or they may drop by to fill out time sheets at the end of the day. For those times when your workers are not out servicing clients — when they are performing activities such as taking inventory or having weekly meetings — an area large enough to accommodate all your employees is an effective way to build relationships among staff.

Depending on your family situation, a separate space for your business, one free from distractions and noise, might be the motivating factor in choosing to rent or purchase commercial space. If your family is receptive and respectful of both the space you establish as your own as well as the time necessary to devote solely to running your business, then a home office should be a serious consideration. If not, the argument for moving off-site is valid.

Drawbacks

When you start your business, finances will be tight. Every penny spent will need to be carefully scrutinized as it may take a weeks or months to clear a profit. You may want to spend your startup capital on items more critical to your business success, like cleaning solutions or equipment. If you cannot afford a commercial space from the start, work it into your goals for the future.

Considerations

If you choose a leased or purchased space intending to have employees use it as a gathering spot before and after jobs, consider the additional space you will need. A break room, reception area, office space, storage areas, and possibly an area for performing maintenance and upkeep on your equipment should figure into your plans.

If a home-based or commercially located business is not the perfect choice for your needs, you can also consider an option where you have a little of both. For example, you may have the right amount of office space in your home but lack storage space for your chemicals and equipment. Perhaps you have plenty of locked space in your garage or basement for the vacuums and other tools but no usable area in your home to dedicate to office space. After a thorough evaluation of your surroundings, purpose, and needs, it is possible you can consider renting an office suite in a business building for the daily managerial tasks and storage of paperwork, or you could opt for establishing your office in your home and rent space in a local warehouse for equipment storage.

The beauty of building your business from the ground up is you get to pick and choose what options best fulfill your needs. Take your time and select thoughtfully — you will be the one living with your decisions.

Organizing Your Office Space

After making the choice of where you will set up your business, think of how you want to set up your office and storage spaces to make the most of your surroundings. Part of the excitement of starting your own business is the result of the energy that builds when your plans begin to come to fruition; you can see your office, your employees, and your business come alive before you.

Heading to the local office supply store or discount furniture and office equipment store can be like a trip to the candy store for business owners. It can fill you with all types of ideas, but resist the urge to purchase everything new for your office and business. Discipline yourself to take stock of your current possessions when locating supplies, furniture, and equipment you will need for your business. Then peruse stores for something new. It is easy to be carried away by new furniture and sparkling equipment, but functionality trumps beauty when it comes to running a business. Business owners can have luck in outfitting their offices with gently used furniture or discontinued models from discount stores, and then put the money they would have spent on new furniture toward cleaning equipment, supplies, or even advertising — areas where their money will make more of a return for their business.

Customers will not visit your business on a regular basis. The bulk of your cleaning work will be done on the client's premises, and you will spend more of your time in their location giving estimates, making service calls and follow-up visits, and performing the cleaning services. While you need to ensure your office setup is clutter-free and organized, spending a bunch of money on furnishings for a waiting area does not make much sense.

Physical Layout

Clients will hardly ever visit your home-based office. The same is true for commercial offices, but you may have clients or vendors who stop by on occasion. For this reason you will want to set up a small reception area. In the reception area, you will want a clean sofa or several chairs, a small table, and good lighting. If you have a receptionist or secretarial staff, it is a good idea to locate this person here to greet visitors and notify you when clients or vendors are waiting to visit with you.

Office Equipment

Even the simplest office arrangement requires a handful of necessary office supplies and equipment to keep the business running and complete daily tasks.

Phones

While you may choose to develop a presence on the Internet for your business, customers will be more likely to contact you via telephone. When starting out, you will want one dedicated land line for your business, even if you work from a home office. You do not want customers to call your home and have someone unfamiliar with your business, such as a visiting relative, answer the phone. If your home and business line are the same, you will lose customers who assume your business lacks professionalism if your voice mail is something like, "John and Mary cannot come to the phone right now..." as opposed to "Thank you for calling Carter's Cleaning Services..." Aside from the fact that you can customize your business line to perform helpful services such as call forwarding and redial that you may not want for your home phone line, having separate lines assures clients that your business is a serious endeavor.

Additional considerations for your land line:

- ✓ A headset or cordless model will allow you or your secretarial staff to perform more than one task (such as locating client paperwork or faxing information) while on the phone with a client or vendor.

- ✓ A toll-free number will help you be competitive if your local market research indicates that competing businesses also have a toll-free number.

- ✓ A meeting with a telephone service representative will give you a good understanding of additional tools and programs the phone company has for small business. You can also discuss options for adding additional lines as your business grows.

In addition to your land line, a cell phone is a wise business investment. A cell phone gives customers and clients immediate access to you at any time for questions, concerns, and requests for services. You can also outfit each cleaning crew supervisor with a cell phone to keep you updated on the status of cleaning jobs, problems and issues, and schedule updates or changes. Business owners may prefer using a pager, but cell phones with voice mail and text message services easily and completely replace the need for pagers at a reasonable cost.

Cell phone companies may offer a plan for small business owners or customers who wish to purchase more than one phone per account. There are also plans for sharing minutes and message services depending on the wireless company and cell phone brand. A visit to your local cell phone store will help you find options in your budget to meet the needs of you and your employees.

Computers

It is virtually impossible to be a successful entrepreneur today without integrating computers into your company. From communications to networking to advertising and maintaining customer, service, and vendor records, a computer is the managerial backbone of your business.

Computers come in all sizes, speeds, colors, and configurations. You may already have a home computer you plan to dedicate for sole use to your business, but be sure it has the capabilities to be a business asset and not a liability. If you have specific questions about choosing the right computer for your business, or if you would just like help selecting the model that best meets the needs of your company, do not hesitate to ask for assistance from sales associates at your local office supply or electronics store. These associates should have the training and knowledge to guide you in the right direction toward a computer that will meet all your needs.

If you are determined to do computer shopping alone, here are relevant guidelines to consider. You will want to choose a machine with at least an 80 GB hard drive to have adequate storage for all your records, files, and graphics; a CD drive to make installation of software programs easy; an adequate number of USB drives; and a current operating system.

There are thousands of software programs available for your business. Quality programs will be crucial to your day-to-day business operations. For your business data you will want to have three types of programs: a word processing program for keying documents, a spreadsheet program for keeping track of financial information, and a graphics/desktop publishing program for creating advertisements and flyers. Word processing programs may also do double-duty as a basic desktop publishing program. This can be an option in the beginning, but if you want to develop brochures and visually appealing advertisements, consider adding the graphics program.

Another software program you will want to look into adding is a financial program. Having all your expenditures and profits available for easy access and updating will save your accountant time and can give you a quick snapshot of the status of your business. Associates at the local office supply store can help, or you might start by asking your accountant or tax preparer if they have a program they prefer to work with. Today's accounting software can import data and records from your bank account directly to your personal computer, a big timesaver.

Printers

Printers have come a long way from the days of dot matrix to provide us with clear, sharp images and professionally printed documents. Technological advances have brought machines to the small business owner that were once only available to large corporations or those willing to pay several thousand dollars for a printer.

Before you start comparing models and prices, think through the types of print jobs you will be performing frequently so that you can make an educated choice on which printer will best meet the demands of your business. Will you be printing only sales records, accounting spreadsheets, and estimate checklists? Are you planning to compile service manuals for your customers, or will you outsource those? What about advertisements, brochures, postcards, flyers, and other promotional items? You can outsource these, but with the correct printer they can be done in your office in smaller batches and customized for your clients.

For basic printing needs — reports, sales figures, and checklists — a black and white printer should suffice. Color printing or enhancement to these documents is a nice touch but unnecessary. If you intend to do the bulk of design and printing of your promotional materials, a color printer is necessary. All color printers can do black and white jobs, but not all black and white printers can do color jobs. Color printer cartridges are more expensive than black and white cartridges; weigh the option of having a black and white printer for routine tasks and a separate color printer for special jobs or promotional materials.

Copiers

Using your printer as a copier to make multiple copies of documents is tempting, but today's printers (with the exception of high volume printers) were not designed for large print jobs. Besides tying up your computer and printer for extended periods of time when you may need access to them for other jobs, using printer ink for copy jobs is more expensive in the long run than investing in a color copier or outsourcing the job to a printing or office supply company.

If your business starts with only you and several employees, you may decide not to invest in a copier. If this is the case, be sure you have easy access to a copier when you need one — for example, if a client needs a second copy of a receipt or estimate or a vendor loses an order form.

Fax Machine

A facsimile machine, commonly called a fax machine, works with a phone line to convert documents and images into electronic signals that can be transmitted to other fax machines. Faxing is a quick and efficient way to send and receive business documents in the amount of time it takes to dial a phone. You will need to fax quotes and contracts to clients, advertisement copy to newspaper editors, and orders to vendors when a written record is required, so a basic fax machine is worth the investment.

Since a fax machine works by transmitting documents over a phone line, you will obviously need a phone line to send and receive data. Businesses commonly have a dedicated fax line — they have one line that connects only to their fax machine. If maintaining a separate line is too costly for your business in the initial stage, you can locate your fax machine near your telephone and swap the connection as needed. Just be certain your phone line is not connected to the fax machine when a potential customer calls ,or they will get a screeching signal when the fax machine picks up instead of a pleasant business voice.

For advice and options on dedicating one phone line to a fax machine, contact the local telephone company you plan to use. They may have a special offer or discount for multiple lines, and they will be able to answer questions directly related to the setup of your business's fax line.

All-In-One Copier and Fax Machine

All-in-one copier and fax machines are integrated machines combining printer, copier, and fax machine features. All-in-one machines are beneficial in that they compact two pieces of equipment into one, saving space in your office. However, all-in-one machines may be limited in their output abilities and are most efficient on smaller print runs. The quality of printed documents from these machines varies, especially if the printer is integrated in the fax part of the machine and not a separate element. Copies may not look professional and crisp, and if the material you will be printing is intended for a customer, you may want to consider other copy options. All-in-ones are a good initial investment, but as your business grows, you will want to upgrade to a copier that can keep up with the demands of your business.

Postage Scales and Meters

When you solicit customers through the mail or when you expand your marketing reach to include homes in a certain geographic area, you will want to consider adding a postage scale, postage meter, or both to your office lineup.

Postage scales measure the weight of mail your company sends out. This includes letters, postcards, and packages. Postage rates are determined by the weight of the item being mailed, and postage scales give an accurate weight reading so you save money by not applying too much postage.

There are two types of postage scales: spring scales and digital scales. If you send primarily letters and a limited number of packages, spring scales are a better, more cost-effective option. Over time, however, the springs can become stretched and render false readings, so be sure to check the spring scale occasionally against a known weight.

Digital scales range in cost and capacity. Today's models may be able to connect directly to a postage meter and print out postage for packages. Others can be linked to your computer and updated with postage and shipping rates from companies like FedEx® and UPS™.

Spring scales cost less — around $40 — whereas digital scales cost hundreds of dollars. Renting from a shipping company or office supply store is also an option for small business owners. Renters normally pay a flat fee per month to use a small postage scale.

If you find your business spending in excess of $50 a month in postage costs, consider adding a postage meter to your standard business equipment. Not only will you save time but you will also be able to print exact postage for all types of mailings, saving your business money.

Before you opt for a postage meter, think through your answers to these questions:

1. How much does your business spend on postage each month?

2. What is the average number of pieces of mail and packages your business ships in a regular day? A busy day?

3. Do you ship primarily pieces of mail (postcards, flyers, letters to clients) or do you routinely ship packages as well?

Postage meters differ from postage scales in that postage meters cannot be purchased. According to federal regulations, postage meters can only be leased. All meters hold pre-determined amounts of postage and print an indicia — the mark that takes the place of a postage stamp — on the item being mailed. Meters can hold up to $1,000 in postage, can be used to meter letters, postcards, and packages, including Priority®, First-Class® and Express Mail®. If you are interested in discount bulk mailing, you will need to apply for a permit through the United States Postal Service® (USPS).

Meters are either traditional or digital. Traditional meters are more costly to maintain, as chips have to be replaced when postage rates change. Digital meters, on the other hand, are electronically updated as the USPS changes rates. Digital meters have the added benefit of printing two-dimensional barcodes, which identifies the sender as well as the destination.

Postage meters can cost between $20 and $50 per month for a basic postage meter machine, plus the cost of postage. Not all meters can handle all sizes of packages — some can only do thin envelopes or postcards, so consider what you will be sending before making the commitment to lease a meter.

Digital Camera

A quality, simple-to-use digital camera is a necessity. One of the best ways to use a digital camera is to take photos of the client's home or business "before" the job and have your client use the photo as a guideline to give exact, detailed instructions to the members of your crew on what services they want performed. Your clients will appreciate the visual reminder of what they want completed, and your crew will have advance notice of the layout and look of the premises before starting a new job.

You can also take "after" photos of large or complex jobs, and share those with your crews as motivation and inspiration, perhaps on a bulletin board or in a thank-you note to them with the photos. Including the photos with the invoice from a large job will remind customers exactly what they paid for and the value of your company's cleaning. If the "before and after" photos are compelling, you may want to ask permission from the client to include them in advertisements, service manuals, or portfolios of your work to share with prospective customers.

Digital cameras range in price from less than $100 to more than $1,000. Choose one with a good zoom lens (4x or higher), large memory capacity (256 MB+) and at least 5 megapixel resolution. Stores may offer free picture printers or color printers as part of a package deal, sale or special offer with digital cameras — so watch for specials and compare prices.

Miscellaneous Office Equipment

Other office machines you may find helpful in making your business office functional:

✓ A paper shredder for sensitive personnel and financial documents

✓ A credit card machine if you choose to take credit cards as a form of payment (More information on credit cards can be found in Chapter 10.)

Vehicle Considerations

Your business success is reliant on the mobility of your cleaning crews and their ability to arrive on location at specified times. You need to make sure every employee has access to reliable transportation.

When deciding which vehicle(s) you will use for your business, select an economical model with a valid warranty, good gas mileage, and enough trunk space to tote all your equipment and supplies to the client's locale.

Take care in keeping your company vehicle clean as it is a direct reflection of your business.

Before you make a final decision on vehicles, however, you will first need to decide if you will transport your crews to the job sites, if you will delegate that responsibility to crew supervisors (for example, all crew members meet at a specified time at your office and the team carpools to the client's site), or if staff members will collectively meet on location via their own mode of transportation.

If you opt to drive your crew or you assign your cleaning crew supervisor to this task, you will need to verify with government authorities what laws you must follow and what responsibilities you incur as the business owner. Be sure the driver (you or the supervisor) contacts their automobile insurance agent to make sure they have the proper coverage for driving your crew. You can find out how best to insure your vehicle, proper usage, and your liability and responsibilities with a call to your insurance agent.

Employees may not have reliable transportation to your office or job sites. This may require you to arrange with public (bus or subway) or private (taxicab) transportation providers to ensure your employees arrive on time.

While not required, emergency vehicle insurance, such as a AAA membership, can be a wise investment for your own vehicle, vehicles in your fleet, or personal vehicles of crew supervisors who drive employees to job sites. You never know when or where you may need it — a flat tire between jobs, a breakdown on the way to a job, client keys accidentally locked inside — but the savings in terms of time, safety, and peace of mind is well worth it.

The use of your personal vehicle for business purposes may entitle you to tax breaks or other financial considerations. Be sure to keep good records and provide these to your accountant or bookkeeper.

Supplies and Suppliers

Before you can comfortably use cleaning products in your clients' homes, you need to know as much about the products, their usage, application, and requirements as possible. An efficient way to go about this is to establish positive relationships with the vendors who sell the products.

Suppliers are valuable assets to your business. When it comes to knowing what products are available to do the best cleaning jobs, vendors are on the front line of the cleaning industry. They have cutting-edge information and insight into which products are hot, which products are not, what solutions and solvents are in demand and, quite simply, what works. Suppliers cater to a wide variety of clients in the cleaning service industry and may know of potential new clients for your business. Cleaning vendors may repay your loyalty to their company by sharing new business leads. They will also know of people interested in becoming employees of your cleaning business. If your relationship gives them the impression that you care for your employees and strive to do your best on every job, they may direct these potential workers to your company.

Finding vendors is not difficult. Begin by scouring the Yellow Pages, newspaper advertisements, trade magazine listings, and getting recommendations from other cleaning business professionals, competitors, and your local Chamber of Commerce. Set up meetings with potential cleaning product suppliers at their place of business so that you can understand how they work and the products they offer.

Establishing Relationships with Vendors

Do not rush into a relationship with a supplier. Take your time when comparing products and vendors. Visit with at least three different vendors. Get to know their product catalogues. Compare their price lists and product offerings. Call to discuss your business, your ideas, and to get suggestions. Visit their offices, and then choose the one who is most helpful and able to deliver the customer service and knowledge you will need.

When you are on good working terms with a vendor, there are ways to get more for your money. One way is to request generic packaging of products you purchase instead of getting name-brand packaging, which costs more. You can also assess the water content of products to make sure you are paying for full-strength product, not a watered-down version. Buy local whenever possible. If this is not available, check with the vendor to see if they have a toll-free number or if they have an online or e-mail ordering system.

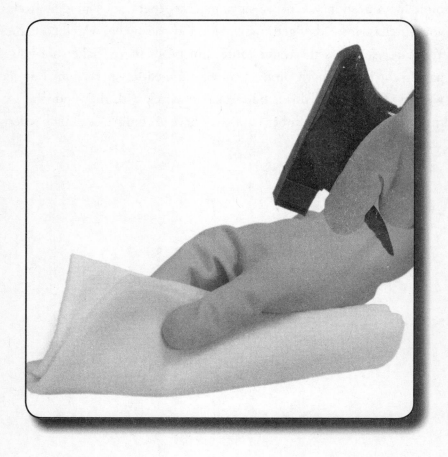

Human Resources

You can spend hours planning and strategizing —working on your business plan, deciding what services to offer, securing financing, establishing your office, and scheduling customers — but without quality employees to make your company stand out, you will fail to get off the ground.

Hiring, retaining, motivating, and rewarding your workers takes time. Your employees are a direct reflection of your business — they are the faces your customers equate with your business — so do all you can to make sure your employees are extensions of yourself. Selecting the right staff is critical to your success.

The application and interview process is not a one-shot deal. Cleaning services have high employee turnover rates due to the physical demands, low pay, and entry-level nature of the job. Use every interview and hiring experience not only to get to know potential employees but also to learn about yourself and the needs of your business.

How Many Employees Do You Need?

There is no "right" number of employees you will need to hire for your business. If you are hoping for a magic formula, you are out of luck. Industry averages and standards can help guide you toward knowing how many workers to add to your business for success.

Determining the proper number of employees with which to start your business relies on several factors:

- ✓ How involved in the actual cleaning will you be? Will you serve as a cleaner and crew leader? Only a crew leader? A backup cleaner? Are you planning to start your cleaning business with only yourself cleaning client homes and businesses? Or do you prefer to hire out all cleaning jobs to crews, leaving you to the administrative tasks of the company?

- ✓ How many clients are you initially serving? Do you have three or four in one section of town that you can service in one day or are they spread out geographically? In the beginning, is it possible to spread out the scheduling of your jobs so they do not all occur at the same time, keeping you free for part of a day to perform office work and to clean for the rest of the day?

- ✓ How large are your cleaning jobs? Homes and residential cleaning jobs are manageable with a smaller number of employees than are janitorial jobs.

Your startup capital will be a major consideration in the number of employees you can initially employ. As your client base and profits grow, you will be able to bring additional employees on board to adequately service all your jobs.

Maid services may begin with the owner serving as a cleaner and hiring additional maids to assist in the cleaning duties. Since maid services occur during daytime business hours, this allows you to clean as well as do office tasks, provided your schedule is properly structured. LaVerne Newton, co-owner of a New York-based cleaning company, Sincerely Chores: Non-Toxic Cleaning for You and Yours, shares that an important lesson she learned was to have employees who were ready to work before they were needed on a job. "We had potential clients book appointments but did not have anyone to service the job. The industry is very competitive, and for new clients to your business, there is no built-in loyalty. You cannot afford to have any delays in the service process if you want to establish your business."

Janitorial companies also start with a small group of employees, either full- or part-time. The difference comes with trying to serve as a cleaner and still keep up with office tasks. Janitorial services clean after-hours. If you spend your nights cleaning, you will want someone to help during the day to maintain business operations. Choose to do all the office work, and you will need to appoint a janitorial crew supervisor. You cannot be in both places and do a decent job, so as owner you will need to make the decision on where your skills and strengths lie.

The number of employees that carpet and upholstery cleaning businesses hire varies based on budgetary considerations, but a good rule of thumb is to have two service technicians per job and one business manager to schedule appointments, answer customer service calls, and perform general office tasks. It is possible to start with one carpet cleaner per job, but having two — one as a senior cleaner, the other as an apprentice — is a valuable timesaver. Moving furniture and equipment, mixing chemicals, cleaning up, and other tasks associated with carpet and upholstery cleaning are completed more quickly with two workers. Customers have a more positive, professional view of cleaning teams with two or more technicians, and saving time on simple tasks leads to additional time to complete other jobs which equals greater profit per team per day.

What Kind of Employee Do You Need?

Potential employees for your cleaning company come from all walks of life. Try to avoid preconceived notions about the type of person who will work best with your business, as you may be pleasantly surprised to find applicants who do not fit that stereotype. Potential employees who work well as cleaners may be these types of people:

- ✓ A regular, consistent worker

- ✓ A team player who enjoys working with others

- ✓ A networker with skills in building and maintaining relationships

- ✓ A parent, college student, or someone with a lifestyle that requires a job with flexible days or hours

- ✓ Active people in good health

- ✓ Independent workers who can complete jobs with little direction

- ✓ Someone who is conscientious and has an eye for detail

- ✓ A person who enjoys cleaning

- ✓ People who respect others and their personal belongings

- ✓ Individuals who reflect their happiness in the quality of their work

More than anything, the ideal employee is one who finds pleasure providing a valuable service and is congenial to both customers and fellow employees.

Where to Search For the Right Employees

Do not limit yourself to thinking only people who are currently out of work or unemployed are looking for jobs. Your ideal employee will be one who seeks a job with your company as a secondary source of income. While you may pay your employees well, income from a cleaning business is not enough to sustain the average employee if it is their sole paycheck.

Think beyond the help-wanted ads in your local newspaper when seeking applicants. Cities and towns may have local or national professional cleaning associations. Contact them to see when and where they meet or if they have a newsletter or other form of communication where you can post an advertisement. Explore the social organizations you are already a part of for possible employees: churches, community groups, school and educational groups, and volunteer organizations. Use these networking opportunities. While the members of these groups may not be looking for additional employment, they have connections outside the main group. If you have left another company or business to start your cleaning business, one option is to mention your budding business to your former colleagues to see if they are interested in part-time work for extra money. Be careful, though, not to "steal" employees from your former employer.

One outstanding place to find potential cleaning crew members is at the local college or university. College students have classes scheduled at odd hours, maybe one class one day and three the next, making them available on a flexible basis. If you get college students who join your company as freshman or sophomores, they will grow with your company and gain experience in the cleaning business as they put themselves through school. Since students normally take classes during the day, their evenings may be free to work for your janitorial company. They will be glad to be able to use you as a reference on their resume, and you will have quality workers to service your clients.

Think also about targeting stay-at-home parents as potential employees. While their children are in school this group of people may be interested in part-time work or having the opportunity to earn extra money.

Advertising for Employees

Just as you advertise for potential clients, you need to advertise for prospective employees. Putting out the word in your social circles that you are searching for workers is not enough to bring in the large pool of applicants you will need.

Advertising for potential service crew members needs to be an ongoing process you can use on a regular basis. Cleaning service businesses suffer from a high rate of turnover, and as your business grows, adding staff members will be critical to your success. Regular members of your cleaning staff will need time off for vacation, illness, and other issues, and you may need to hire additional employees as reinforcements.

Advertising for employees can take a number of forms. One suggestion is to keep an ongoing help wanted advertisement in your local paper. Running a recurring advertisement every three to four months will ensure potential employees are reached on an ongoing basis. Another idea is to make posters or flyers with tear-off tabs containing your business name and phone number. These can be posted in a number of locations:

✓   Employment centers

✓   Grocery stores

✓ Campus billboards

✓ Coin laundries

✓ Community buildings

After asking permission to post your announcement, check back frequently to make sure there are adequate supplies of your information for new possible workers.

When starting your business, you might be tempted to hire family and friends, but consider this carefully before acting on the temptation. Unless your cleaning business is intended to serve as a family cleaning business, understand that there are numerous stories of ruined friendships and relationships between new business owners and friends and family. Making the transition from a casual relationship to one of employee/ employer requires changes people can find difficult to make. You might realize that family members cannot take orders well from you or do not consider your requests as serious ones. Acquaintances may assume they are entitled to special treatment from you as well. If you choose to hire friends or family, be ready for the possible complications from the onset of their employment.

Case Study: Elizabeth Solo

Tailor Maid, Inc.

Boca Raton, FL

www.tailormaid.com

Elizabeth Solo, owner

Without steady, reliable, and detail-oriented workers, a cleaning company cannot be successful. Clients will come and go for a number of reasons, but establishing a strong core of good employees who like cleaning and want to work for your company for years to come is the real secret of thriving in the cleaning industry.

Case Study: Elizabeth Solo

Providing cleaning services to clients is an intimate relationship. Trust is the number one factor in the client/cleaner relationship, and constant turnover of the cleaning staff makes building relationships difficult. Clients do not like a changes in the people they are inviting to their homes, so build client trust in your company by providing them with the same cleaners whenever possible.

Finding good people to work for you can be difficult, and you may have to overlook their shortcomings to keep them. Treating workers well so they want to continue working for you is important as the positive relationship you build with employees will eventually trickle down to their job performance and relationships with clients.

Keeping workers happy involves a number of elements. Knowing they have a consistent work schedule and are servicing clients they care for is one important element; being paid well is another. Trying to please employees requires energy and work, but it is better than the alternative of having a cleaning job to finish and having an employee quit on the spot, leaving you with no one to service the client.

If you love what you do, are passionate about the job, and instill this into the employees who represent your company, success will follow.

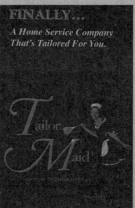

The Interview Process

Before starting the interviewing process, you will need to know what jobs you will be hiring for and determine the requirements for those jobs. This includes creating job descriptions for all the positions you will be staffing. Common initial positions you will want to include are:

✓ Entry-level cleaning crew member

✓ Cleaning crew supervisor

✓ Office/secretarial staff

✓ Marketer or advertising specialist

✓ Any specialized position your company needs

Writing job descriptions might seem a tedious task, but there are at least three good reasons for putting your employee expectations into writing:

✓ Having a written list of expectations for possible employees helps to weed out less-than-qualified applicants who do not meet your needs, saving you interview time.

✓ The description reminds you of the qualities and skills you require of your workers in order to run an effective and efficient business.

✓ It clearly states your expectations for all employees from the start so they are clear on the terms of employment.

At the same time you are compiling your job descriptions, you will want to think about your pay rates and what your employees can expect to make; applicants will want to know your company's pay scale during the interview. The best way to develop competitive pay rates is to research the pay scales of local competing cleaning companies to determine a minimum and maximum; then create wage rates for each of the jobs you will be interviewing for or will interview for in the future. Consider paying more for employees with previous cleaning experience and for those you hire or promote to cleaning crew supervisor. You can find out this information by calling local cleaning companies, introducing yourself as a new business owner and sharing that you would like to talk to them about their pay rates. See the Pay Scale Research Sheet in Appendix B for helpful information for your decision-making process.

Application Forms

The application form is the first step for every applicant. If you choose to hire your children or other family, friends, or acquaintances, having each applicant complete a form eliminates potential problems down the road. Each person you hire to work for you needs the same kind of documentation and records in their personnel folder to avoid potential claims of favoritism and discrimination. The signature on each application is your assurance that if the applicant has lied or provided false information of any sort on the application, you have the legal right to terminate their employment at any time. Information provided on the application can also provide verification of resume credentials. Do not hire an applicant based solely on the merits they list on a resume; require them to fill out an application so you have legal backing to look into their claims.

You are not required to interview every person who fills out an application form. Instead, consider the form a screening tool. Use it as a snapshot view of applicants to determine if they have had the experience or the skills for which you are hiring.

Basic employment applications are available at office supply stores. This is an easy, efficient method of creating an application form. If you want a more personalized version, perform an Internet search on application forms and compile your own form based on questions that meet your specific qualifications. If you invent your own form, be sure to have a legal expert look it over to make certain you are in compliance with employment laws. Appendix B contains a Sample Application Form for your use or modification.

Interview Questions

The interview is your chance to ask open-ended questions of applicants to determine if they are a good fit for your company. You will need to ask certain types of questions to get the information that will help you in making a decision about the abilities, skills, and knowledge of your potential employees.

It is impossible to know from the start if each person you choose to hire will be an outstanding employee for your company or if you will have to address problems later with formal reprimands or termination. Creating insightful interview questions, however, is a chance for you to ask questions to give you enough information to make educated decisions on which applicants might suit your business.

The goal of the interview questions you construct is to get the applicant to reveal as much about themselves as possible. To accomplish this, your questions must get them to open up through conversation.

Good interview questions:

✓ Are open-ended, requiring interviewees to elaborate on themselves, give examples of their previous experience, personality, and work ethic

✓ Are not yes/no type questions or easily answered with a simple statement or phrase

✓ Avoid any subject that would violate human rights laws, including information regarding race, religion, marital status, age, disability, or gender

✓ Provide interviewees the chance to share what they have done in other jobs or in life experiences that applies to your business

Every applicant you interview should get the same list of questions. Being consistent with your list will give you a sense for the type of replies from applicants that make better employees for your business. A list of sample interview questions is provided in Appendix B, Sample Interview Questions. Use these as a guideline or create your own. To be sure your questions are appropriate and within the boundaries of applicable laws, have your lawyer check them before you interview anyone.

The Interview Itself

If you are nervous about conducting interviews, imagine how nervous your applicants are. Being in the interview chair is more intimidating than asking questions. You will have plenty of chances to interview people interested in working for you if an applicant does not pan out, but this may be their only chance to represent themselves and their abilities to you.

Do your best to relax the interviewees. Getting to know them on a more personal level is your mission; grilling them about previous employment and work experience is not. Make them comfortable and put them at ease to facilitate openness and honesty. Remove from the interview environment any elements that might make them hesitant or unable to focus.

After you are both settled, begin asking your questions. Print out a copy of the questions to use as a guideline and a place to write down responses. Go with the flow of the interview; do not rush to the next question. Give applicants time to think about their answers and formulate a response, then probe their answers with further questions. Do not stray far with side conversations — your list of questions should guide your interview. Your job is to ask questions, listen to their responses, note their body language and the interest with which they reply, and record their answers for future reflection and comparison with other applicants.

After you have asked all your questions, share your job description with the interviewee. Encourage them to ask questions so that they clearly understand your expectations and tasks required. Clarify company policies and treat applicants to a favorable impression of you, your business and operations so even if you choose not to hire them, they will be more likely to share their positive feelings with others outside your business.

In wrapping up the interview, tell them what to expect from you in terms of the hiring schedule and process. Tell them when they can they expect a phone call to let them know if you have chosen them. Advise them if it is okay for them to contact you to see if their qualifications meet your needs. Let them know if you will call to hire them or to request a second interview. Thank them for the chance to interview them, and do not forget to ask permission to check the references they listed on their application form.

Post Interview Considerations

As soon as possible after the interview, take time to review your notes and record your impressions of the candidate. To get a complete picture of the applicant, reflect on these elements of the interview:

✓ Was the applicant well-groomed? Not taking pride in their appearance may be an indication that details are not a priority for them.

✓ Did the interviewee make regular eye contact? Did they smile? As much as you schedule to avoid it, employees and clients will inevitably come in contact. You want every element of your service to reflect positively back to your business, even in times of stress.

✓ Did the applicant exhibit basic manners and common courtesy?

✓ Were any of your questions overly difficult for the applicant to answer? If there was more than one, do these questions have anything in common?

✓   What sense did you get from the interviewee's behavior and body language? Note any positive or negative impressions you noted during your interaction.

A Post-Interview Notes worksheet is provided in Appendix B for ease in documenting the details of each interview.

Check on the references supplied by your applicants. You may be able to glean interest insights and perspectives from former employers and business contacts. At the least, verify the truth of the applicant's previous employment and reasons for leaving. Character and personality traits you discover may be more valuable than actual work experience.

Document each step in the hiring process for each employee from application to interview to hiring (or reasons for choosing not to hire an applicant). Lawsuits filed on behalf of disgruntled applicants or angry employees are becoming common in the business world. Accurate, detailed records are your best guard against claims of racism, sexism, or other issues that may lead to a law suit. A sample worksheet for documenting the hiring process is in Appendix B.

When it comes down to making the decision of which applicants to hire, a good rule of thumb is to hire those you feel comfortable with and would trust in your own home. Be selective and take time to make an informed decision, as your choices will put your company's reputation — and future — on the line.

Occasionally evaluate your hiring process to be sure it meets your needs and is successful in helping you employ the right type of workers. Jobs change, markets evolve, and workers grow; it makes sense that your hiring process will, too. If you discover a recurring issue or feel that you need to expand your process, think about these questions:

1. Are your interview questions clear, and do they lead applicants toward giving you a valid response that will help you make a decision?

2. Do your questions reflect the information you need to hire the right people?

3. Does the applicant do much of the talking during the interview process?

4. Are your job descriptions and company policies clear?

5. Did you make a positive initial impression and leave the applicant with a good feeling about your company?

6. Is there anything you can do differently to help hire qualified applicants?

For more help in the interviewing and hiring process, check out *501+ Great Interview Questions for Employers and The Best Answers for Prospective Employees* from Atlantic Publishing.

Legal Considerations

In your role as an employer, you have legal obligations to follow in the hiring process. You need to be aware of and up-to-date on local, state, and federal laws regarding hiring, termination, compensation, taxes, and related issues.

Employee and Employer Rights

Your employees are granted specific rights based on the state in which you live and your business resides. Local employment offices are the best place for you to begin gathering information on what responsibilities you have as an employer toward your workers. Consult these experts before hiring for advice on creating employee policies, procedures, job descriptions and pay rates. As a business owner, you need to adhere to all the laws and regulations regarding every person you hire as well as what you can legally expect from your workers.

When you visit your local labor office, you will need to find out specific details on these issues in particular:

✓ Minimum wage

✓ Hours of work

✓ Health and safety laws governing the workplace and job sites

✓ Human rights issues

✓ Employer tax for social benefits

✓ Rest periods and meal breaks while on the job

✓ Full-time, part-time, and contractual employees' rights, responsibilities, and obligations

✓ Sick leave

✓ Worker's compensation

✓ Vacation pay

✓ Maternity and/or parental leave

✓ Statutory holidays

✓ Termination policies

Child Labor Laws

If you anticipate hiring teenagers (youths aged 18 and younger) for any length of time and for any position within your cleaning business, you need to know how child labor laws impact the hours and types of jobs they are legally allowed to do. Provisions within the Fair Labor Standards Act were created to protect the educational opportunities of minors and prohibit their working under adverse conditions that could affect their health and well-being.

Basic child labor guidelines apply teenagers you hire from your local area and youth in your own family — including your own children. At any age, your children may work for you in your cleaning business as long as you are the sole proprietor and follow all other age-related laws.

The minimum legal age for work is 16, but you can employ 14- and 15-year-old youths outside school hours under restricted conditions. Additional guidelines include:

✓ 18-year-olds and above can work unlimited hours

✓ 16- and 17-year-olds can perform any non-hazardous job (as defined by the Secretary of Labor) for unlimited hours

✓ 14- and 15-year-olds can perform any non-hazardous job outside school hours — three hours or less per school day, 18 hours or less per week, 8 hours per non-school day, and 40 hours per non-school week. Work hours for this group must be between the hours of 7 a.m. and 7 p.m. During the summer (June 1 to Labor Day), these hours extend to 7 a.m. to 9 p.m.

When employing anyone under the age of 19, keep detailed records on all aspects of their involvement in your business. Start with documented records of date of birth in their personnel files, and an age or employment certificate. Use a log to record the start and end times of each day they work for you, a list of tasks completed, and a tally of daily and weekly hours. See Appendix B for a sample Youth Work Log.

Keeping Employees Happy and Productive

Unlike a retail business or restaurant, when you own a cleaning business, you are selling service to the client. The sole providers of this service — the representation of your company — comes down to one thing: your employees. Employees are more than workers; they are your business.

Taking Care of Employees to Get the Most from Them

Your business is only as strong and productive as your employees are. Cleaning businesses are particularly vulnerable to a high rate of employee turnover. Do your best to treat every employee with respect, recognize their individual contributions to your company, and show them how much you value them on a regular basis to keep your turnover rates manageable.

One way to increase loyalty and satisfaction is to offer a benefit package. Providing insurance, whether medical, dental, vision, or a combination of all three, may be a difficult prospect in the initial stages of your business, as insurance premiums increase every year. However, developing employee loyalty through benefits shows employees that you care about them and their health.

A second way to set your business apart is through compensation. You do not need to pay ridiculously high hourly rates to make a difference to employees; establishing a pay scale slightly higher than the minimum pay rates in your area is a simple way to set yourself apart. Consider giving employees time off with pay based on performance or goals achieved, and work out incentive plans to give your employees motivation to do tasks well. Structure your bonus and incentive plan around the jobs your employees perform each day. Possible reasons to reward employees include:

✓ Number of jobs completed (by day, week, month, or year) satisfactorily

✓ Years of service

✓ Service as trainers and/or crew leaders

✓ Commendations from clients

✓ On-time consistency for jobs

✓ Perfect attendance over a given time

✓ Recruitment of new customer accounts

Building loyalty is crucial in tipping the scales in favor of your business to give employees no reason to look elsewhere for employment. Rewarding employees does not have to be expensive, either. Perhaps you can swap services with local businesses (i.e. a local restaurant might exchange gift certificates for free cleaning services). Hosting lunches and parties, even group pot lucks are a good way to build staff morale. Time off for jobs well done, even if it is minimal, is an employee favorite. Gift cards, recognition stickers for nametags, and featuring an employee of the week, month, or year are also popular options. For additional ways to motivate your workers, check out *365 Ways to Motivate and Reward Your Employees Everyday with Little or No Money* from Atlantic Publishing.

When Trouble Strikes

No matter how well you prepare your workers for their jobs, problems are bound to happen. There are a variety common issues you may deal with as the owner of a cleaning business, and you may need these suggestions on how to handle them.

Injury and First Aid

Even a minor injury affecting an employee impacts productivity, jobs completed, and customer satisfaction — all negatives in terms of helping your business succeed.

Training sessions are a prime opportunity to share with employees established procedures to follow in case of injuries. With any serious injury employees should seek immediate medical attention. For less severe situations, equip each of your cleaning crews with a first aid kit including sterile gloves, bandages, bandaging tape, gauze pads or strips, alcohol pads, antibiotic ointment, eye wash solution, and a small pair of scissors. Make your crew leader responsible for keeping the kits stocked and available on every job site.

Take time to familiarize yourself with the worker's compensation and employer liability for injuries regulations for your state. Knowing your rights and responsibilities as an employer before the information is necessary will help you implement the proper policies and procedures for on-the-job injuries and keep you prepared ahead of time.

Breakage

Your bonding insurance company will have specific guidelines to follow on the proper procedure for reporting breakage of client items, and you will need to conduct your own investigation into the matter to provide the necessary information.

Your clients may be understanding of the accident or like the cleaner. In this instance, a replacement of the item may be a satisfactory solution, but if the item was sentimental or valuable, you will need to reimburse the client and report the incident to your insurance company. Expect to absorb the cost of loss and pay the deductible.

Keep careful documentation of all instances of breakage and review them regularly. If they are occurring regularly to the same staff, consider replacing them with workers who are more careful.

Theft

Theft affects more than the person from whom the object is stolen; it affects your profits, company image, and staff morale. Clients hire cleaners as strangers in their home. Establishing trust comes with time, and if that bond is violated, relationships may be irrevocably broken.

Enact common-sense policies to reduce the temptations of theft. Employees should not be allowed to carry any type of personal item such as a purse or bag with them into a client's home. They can store these items in a locked location at your business or leave them locked in their car or company vehicle. Provide adequate supervision by yourself in the beginning and later by trusted crew supervisors. Make sure employees understand that the consequence of theft is immediate termination.

If you discover employee theft, act quickly, confidentially, and carefully to address the situation. Sharing the information before the matter is resolved satisfactorily opens you up to potential legal action from those involved, even if the incident was a mistaken assumption. You should interview witnesses or others who have knowledge of the situation. You may be able to get surveillance tape from clients who have home security systems. Interview everyone associated with the event, including the accused person without implicating anyone. Inform employees that the questioning process is not to be shared with anyone outside the investigation, as this is a legal matter.

Do not ask pointed, direct questions. Instead, probe for knowledge of the situation. Insist on facts, not assumptions. Document the findings of your questioning, and keep this documentation separate from employee records in a secure place, especially in case legal action may be necessary. Do not accuse an employee until you have come to a positive conclusion.

If the incident of stealing is confirmed, take swift action by terminating the employment of the worker in question. To complete an investigation and discover misconduct without subsequent punishment damages the morale of your staff and lessens their view of you as a competent, fair employer.

Depending on the seriousness of the theft, you may need to involve local law enforcement. However, consider this action seriously. Negative publicity, loss of clients, staff, and profits may result. Weigh the incident carefully before choosing to notify authorities.

Lack of Performance

If you determine employees are not meeting your expectations — whether they are late to jobs, leaving jobs incomplete, or interacting in an unprofessional manner with clients or other employees — have a talk with the employee. Keep a log in the employee's file documenting each instance of unsatisfactory performance or behavior and the results of your interaction with them regarding the incident. Indicate what they plan to do to remedy the behavior or how they intend to improve. If you discover yourself meeting with an employee more than once or twice, reconsider their employment. Spending time with them continuously discussing their poor performance takes your time from running your business and their time from cleaning. Establish a written procedure for dealing with this issue, and implement it in the employee handbook for workers to be familiar with as they are trained and hired.

Training

Reasons for Training

Your business is represented by your employees. You want to put your best workers out for the public to see. You need to see how even your experienced cleaners do what they do to make sure it reflects well on your business and meets your standards.

Whatever the focus of your training, good training takes time — both to plan and to implement. However, time spent training will pay off. Sending your workers to the homes of your clients without adequate knowledge of their jobs and expectations is detrimental to your company's success.

Logistics of Training Sessions

Before your employees gather for the training sessions, you will need to figure out the logistics of those meetings. Use these questions to lay the groundwork:

1. Where will the training be held? While you may have available space in your business location to host a gathering of your employees, you may have a higher rate of success if it is possible to demonstrate cleaning techniques and have employees model instructions in a real-life setting. Seek out a willing friend or client to trade the use of their home as a training site in return for a free cleaning. Perhaps a property manager would do the same

with a vacant apartment, condominium, or model home. If your business cannot accommodate your staff, there are meeting rooms at local libraries, retail businesses, and even churches that you can schedule for free in advance.

2.   Based on the content of your training session, different locations might be more conducive to your purposes. Choose a location that will help your session be as productive as possible.

Scheduling Training

Ensure employee knowledge and procedures meet with your company's criteria by requiring every employee, regardless of previous experience, to attend every training session. Require employees to make up trainings they miss. To be fair, inform your employees well in advance of dates, times, expectations, and other necessary details of the upcoming training. The best way to do this is to create an agenda with relevant information and give it to your employees so they know what is coming.

Training Leaders

In the beginning, the responsibility for leading the training sessions will fall on you. If you have other partners or key leaders in your company, they may also fill the role. Be sure you are all on the same page and are thoroughly versed and knowledgeable of the expectations, techniques, and methods, so the message of the training sessions is consistent.

You may over time discover one of your staff members has solid presentation skills or is a good group leader. "I am fortunate that my partner Michael A. Cleveland can motivate a snowman to buy snow. His personality will not allow a training session to be less than enjoyable," says Sincerely Chores co-owner LaVerne Newton. "Our trainings are also successful because our team is family. We have high expectations, but we also realize that our employees have families, other obligations, and other jobs. We make it a habit to keep our tone light yet stern."

Delegating certain aspects of the training to others may also work. Weigh this carefully as you will still need to be present for the trainings. Variety in presentations and presenter styles keeps employees engaged and interested, but the content should be the focus.

Setting Up a Training Session

After the logistics of training are squared away, decide what type of training you will be offering. Employee training sessions normally fall into one of three broad categories:

1. Orientation for new employees, where the focus will be company policy, procedures, and expectations

2. Service training built on how-to, hands-on activities for employees to learn proper cleaning techniques, familiarize themselves with equipment, supply and product usage, and explicit instructions on how to complete all the tasks expected of them when servicing clients

3. Developmental training, which builds on the skills and strengths of your workers to improve performance, morale, and the ability to meet challenges successfully

Every training you conduct needs to be pre-planned and contain the following elements for success:

Objectives

What are the goals of your training? Writing down your training objectives not only guides you toward developing the best method of teaching the objectives to your workers, but also gives employees a clear list of expected outcomes. It shows exactly what you want from them.

Activities

The point of any type of training you lead is the same: for your employees to learn the material you are teaching. In a perfect world, everyone would acquire knowledge in the same way, but that is not the way it works.

Every person learns differently. Your employees may pick up information easily from listening or they may prefer reading. Incorporate a variety of activities over the course of the training to get all employees motivated and involved. Observe your workers to get a feel for how they learn best. They may be able to share with you how they learn. Provide a variety of methods — verbal explanations, worksheets, or visual demonstrations — to help everyone get the most out of your message.

Scenarios

All the training in the world is inadequate if your workers lack the skills or confidence to satisfactorily perform their jobs. Giving them the opportunity to practice their new behaviors or procedures before they go back to their work sites will help build their self-esteem and give them a foundational competency from which to work.

Scenarios are not limited to how employees can deal with customers, though that is an excellent way to teach positive interaction skills. Scenarios where workers take what you have taught them and demonstrate (with guidance and prompting if necessary) their comprehension and ability to complete the task are the heart of training.

Scenarios can be individual (how to assemble a vacuum cleaner or polish silver) or with a partner (interpersonal skills with clients and other employees). Activities and training content can even be arranged as a group activity — brainstorming ways to streamline cleaning techniques without sacrificing quality, for example.

Whatever type of scenario you introduce in your trainings, make it fun, not intimidating. People may be uncomfortable role-playing, so consider alternatives for these folks to learn the same content in a more relaxed manner. If employees do not like role-playing in a group setting, their minds will be focused on their discomfort instead of the content you are teaching.

To help you plan your training sessions, a Training Planning Session worksheet is included in Appendix B.

Handbook of Company Policies and Procedures for Employees

Even with thorough and comprehensive training, employees will have questions. Consider compiling an employee handbook to keep your important documents in one place for employees to refer to when needed. Even if it is only a handful of pages long, making employees responsible for finding their own answers to common problems is a skill you should encourage. A good employee handbook should include:

Daily Operations and Expectations

✓ When and where to report for work — Thirty minutes before the job starts? Ten minutes? On time? At the office? On the job site? At a common location?

✓ Job Descriptions — Include copies of all the jobs in your company in this section.

✓ Who to contact in the company for issues they may encounter

- ✓ Days off for sickness

- ✓ Running late/tardiness

- ✓ Scheduling time off in advance

- ✓ Upcoming job schedules

Uniform/Dress Codes

Implementing a dress code or creating a uniform policy is not required, but there are benefits to having your employees wear standard uniforms to represent your cleaning business. These benefits can include:

- ✓ Making employees easily identifiable to clients

- ✓ Improving morale among your staff

Within your employee handbook, specify whether uniforms must be worn. If you allow employees to wear something besides a uniform, consider the following:

- ✓ Tee shirts with jeans or knit pants are a good, cost-efficient alternative to uniforms.

- ✓ Specify the quality and condition of the clothes to be worn to job sites: no holes, tears, or excessively frayed hems.

- ✓ Clothing needs to fit in a way that allows employees to perform their work well. Excessively loose clothing is an occupational hazard: an oversized shirt can catch on handles or items and tear or break the item. Clothing that is too tight will not be as comfortable as needed to allow employees to complete their tasks.

✓ Smocks or aprons can also be a cost-effective alternative to full uniforms.

✓ Rubber soled, non-slip shoes may be something you wish to require.

✓ Nametags add to the professional image of your staff in the eyes of the customer and give staff a sense of being valued. If employees are required to wear nametags, include this in your policy.

If you do require and provide uniforms, decide your uniform policy in advance. Spell these policies out in your handbook to eliminate any confusion.

✓ Will each employee be provided with two or three shirts and be expected to purchase additional shirts as needed?

✓ Will you supply employees with a new shirt on a regular basis?

✓ Will you provide a clothing allowance in employee paychecks and expect them to take care of the maintenance and upkeep of their clothing?

✓ Will you provide nametags? Are employees required to wear nametags?

Company Policies

Company policies questions an employee might have about working for your company. Policies on everything from basic issues such as lunch times to complex ones like benefits give employees notice of your policies up front and in writing to avoid complications later. Key elements of your daily operations and expectations should be backed by policies.

Company policies you may want to include are:

✓   Work hours and lunch breaks

✓   Performance expectations

✓   Going against policies

✓   Processes for requesting time off

✓   Suspected and confirmed cases of theft from clients or your company

✓   Benefits information

✓   Grievances against co-workers

✓   Substance abuse policy

✓   Sexual harassment policy

✓   Smoking policy

✓   Confidentiality agreements

✓   Client interaction policy

✓   Promotional policy/requirements

In Appendix B, you will find an extensive, detailed outline containing all the elements of the employee handbook you will need to address.

8

Growing Your Business through Marketing

A solid marketing plan can be the difference between businesses that grow, prosper, and bring in customers and those who do not. Creating a marking strategy — including the how, why, and who you want to reach — is not difficult. The first step is figuring out who you want to reach, your target market.

Target Your Market

Before printing your first flyer, know the market niche you want to target. In the process of compiling your business plan, you may have already determined the niche you want to tailor your business toward. You will have made choices regarding residential or janitorial services, the number of customers you want to serve (including the target geographical area), and the types of services you want to offer.

Create Your Image

Decide what you want the first thought to be when a customer hears your company name. If you are familiar with the needs of your market you will know the type of client you want to attract to your business. This will help you know what types of services they desire. Consider this in every step of image development.

Your business image includes everything associated with your name as seen by potential clients. This applies to visuals, such as your company logo, stationery, marketing communications literature, and advertisements. It includes your staff, their physical presence, business etiquette, social interaction skills, and service ability. Even things you may not think of — like the cleanliness of your equipment and vehicles, your reputation and integrity, and your license, bonding, and insurance policies — have an impact on your business image. Since your initial clients may come to you as a result of your advertisements and presence in the community, put your best face forward to create an inviting, pleasant business image they will want in their homes and offices.

Your business' name is also a crucial part of your business's image. Choosing a name that gives clients a picture of your business is a first step in establishing a clear, positive image for potential customers. Without it, clients will not be willing to take a chance on your services.

To order your thoughts and guide your planning, an Image and Logo Planning worksheet is included in Appendix B.

Advertising Strategy and Plan

It is critical that you properly plan your marketing strategy before signing up your first client. Your advertising strategy is similar to your business plan in that it needs to be created under non-stressful circumstances — while you have the time to think through details and are able to choose advertising strategies that meet the needs of your business. The initial time spent planning will pay off in saved time, money, stress, and aggravation because you will have a plan to fall back on when you need it most. Last minute or hurried planning can lead to misinformed choices that seem good at the time but may require even more time, money, and effort to undo.

Having a plan will guide your advertising decisions so that if you discover one method of advertising is not working for your company, you can change, modify, or even replace it with another strategy that brings in more business. Repeatedly spending money and time on advertising that does not accomplish the goal, which is to build your client base, is detrimental to your success.

The easiest way to gather information on which advertising strategies work best to draw the type of customer you want to attract is simple: ask the customer. When they call about your services, ask how they heard about your services. Were they referred by a current customer, family member, or business associate? Did they receive your postcard in the mail or a flyer on their doorstep? Did your radio or television advertisement make them curious? Was your Web site informative enough? If you include coupons in your marketing plan, you can code them to trace the publication where they were published. You may discover that a fair number of your clients are interested because of a Yellow Pages ad or because they are readers of a specific newspaper section; you can increase your advertising energy and spending in that area instead of wasting it in another.

Your advertising strategy is built on promoting your business in a variety of places and ways:

✓   Company literature

    ✓ Business cards

- ✓ Flyers

- ✓ Stationery

✓ Printed advertisements

- ✓ Newspapers

- ✓ Yellow Pages

- ✓ Business directories

✓ Customer service contact and calls

✓ Networking with other businesses

✓ Community involvement

Common business knowledge says that the average customer needs to see a visual representation of your business three times in three different ways before they choose your services. Making the most of your advertising strategies does make a difference.

Case Study: Bill Weaver

Maid For You New York, Inc.

Long Island City, NY

www.maidforyounewyork.com

Bill Weaver, District Manager

In the initial stages of starting a maid service, it can be tempting to forgo the research into the type of clientele you want your business to attract. After all, there are other details to attend to and tasks to be completed. It may seem a waste of time.

Case Study: Bill Weaver

Knowing where to spend your hard-earned money to get the most for your advertising and marketing dollars, however, is one of the easiest and best ways to grow your client base. Maid services appeal to busy, working folks in the late-30s to mid-50s age group who have discretionary income, so advertising on radio stations that cater to this age group has been an overwhelmingly successful strategy for Maid For You New York, Inc.

Advertisements of All Kinds

There are several things you need to include in your advertisements to make them successful at drawing in clients. Every marketing message you create should contain three necessary pieces of information:

1. Who you are (your business name)

2. What you do

3. How customers can contact you

A fourth element you may consider adding is how your services can improve a customer's life. You will not be able to include this on all advertisements but if you create two or three standard lines ("Richie's Cleaning gives you more time to spend with the people you love" or "Give yourself the gift of clean with Richie's Cleaning Services"), you can add them to advertisements as space allows.

Three Types of Advertisements

Business advertisements normally fall into one of three broad categories. You may want to try a little of each type in the beginning to see how well your customer base responds and make changes to your plan as needed.

Traditional Advertisements

Traditional advertisements are the backbone of successful advertising strategies. They include a variety of media to reach your target market.

Yellow Pages

The average cost to market your business in the Yellow Pages is $700 to $3,000 per year, depending the type of advertisement you choose. If you choose to use the Yellow Pages, consider the following observations:

- ✓ A simple and effective method of advertising

- ✓ Can list your business name or run an advertisement

- ✓ Choice of black and white or color

- ✓ May be able to get a discount for advertising in the Yellow Pages when you sign up for an additional business phone line

- ✓ Can be a good place for larger companies but not necessarily smaller ones because the advertisement continues to run even when you have a full client schedule

- ✓ Fees for listing and advertising in the Yellow Pages run higher in larger cities

Newspapers

- ✓ Inexpensive and flexible to the needs of the business owner

- ✓ An excellent tool for targeting a specific geographic market

- ✓ Requires a little careful consideration when placing an advertisement for maximum effectiveness

You have two options if you choose to advertise in newspapers:

Classifieds

- ✓ Expensive, as papers charge by the word

- ✓ Less popular for potential clients seeking services with the advent of the internet

Display Advertisements

- ✓ Add an extra visual prompt to customers when they see your advertisement

- ✓ Can be black and white or color

Do a little preliminary research through newspaper sections to find where advertisements similar to yours run. Requesting placement of your ad in a particular section of the paper costs a bit more, but being in the wrong place can make potential customers miss your business entirely.

Flyers

Marketing flyers are easy and inexpensive to produce but are also easily thrown away. In addition, flyers hung on a doorknob may seem appealing and cost-effective, but they can attract attention to empty homes. This is a nuisance for the homeowner when arriving home and could reflect negatively on your business.

Careful targeting of potential clients with flyers can be an outstanding marketing strategy. Areas you may want to target include:

- ✓ Homes in new developments

- ✓ Homes being moved into or out of

- ✓ Vacant apartments or condominiums

You may also want to consider posting flyers in common public areas if the clientele have an interest in and are able to afford your services. Select places where active people meet, group, or frequently visit:

- ✓ Gyms and workout facilities

- ✓ Grocery stores

- ✓ School offices

- ✓ Break rooms or lunch rooms in retail buildings

- ✓ Community Centers

- ✓ Hospitals

- ✓ Churches

As with all your advertising materials, verify with owners or management on the premises that it is acceptable to them that you post your flyers.

Make the flyer attractive and uncluttered. No one has time to decipher your message if it is not clear.

Direct Mail

Direct mail advertisements are individual marketing pieces such as postcards, flyers, or letters sent in the mail to every home or business in a targeted geographic area. Direct mail may cost only pennies per piece.

Visit your local Post office and talk to a clerk about the number of businesses and or homes in your selected area to get a feel for the overall size and population of the area. They can give you specific demographic information to help you determine if the area is too large or small for the needs of your business. They can also give you detailed breakdowns of neighborhoods if you are interested in further limiting your advertisements to select clientele.

One way to approach direct mail is to send your advertisement to a large but specific area and then gather information from clients who respond to narrow the scope for future advertising campaigns.

Mail Packs

Mail packs are a version of direct mail — except that instead of sending your advertisement alone it is sent in a common envelope known as a "pack." It is packaged with other advertisements from different businesses. You can include in your advertisement in a mail pack an incentive for customers to call your business, such as a coupon or percentage off basic services.

Mail packs are less expensive than direct mail but have two major drawbacks:

1. Mail packs may not target all potential customers in your

pre-determined sales area (or inadvertently reach clients living in an area in which you do not intend to offer services)

2. The company issuing the mail packs is the sole determinant of what additional advertisements go into the mail pack with yours. The company controls where and when the pack is distributed.

Social Advertising

Whereas traditional advertising focuses on printed materials, social advertising relies on human interaction to draw clients to your business. The main players in this method may be you, your partners, or even someone you hire specifically for marketing purposes. What is important is the face-to-face contact this person gives to customers in representing your business and services.

Successful social advertising requires an ability to talk comfortably with others about your services. If you are nervous, shy, or hesitant about public speaking, build your confidence through role-playing with a trusted associate until you are prepared to interact with new clients. There are also books and other materials that can help develop the self-confidence you need to advocate for your business.

There are only four main types of social advertising, but together they have the potential to bring the greatest number of clients to your business.

Word of Mouth

Considered the single best method of advertising for the cleaning industry, word of mouth is highly recommended for one reason: it is free. Word of mouth comes from doing jobs well, conducting yourself with integrity, and giving the client everything they expect. Customers may not tell your workers they have done an outstanding job, but they will tell someone else, including friends, family, and coworkers.

Small businesses may rely exclusively on word-of-mouth referrals to build their client base. One way to encourage your customers to refer your business to others is through a referral rewards system. For example, if a new customer seeks your service because they were referred by a current client, reward the referring client with a free cleaning or additional service on your next visit. At the least, be sure to thank the referring customer for their loyalty. Your company grow, and you will demonstrate to your employees how important it is for them to do their best. Cleaning performed to client expectations is a calling card in itself. Do good work, and your clients will do the advertising for you.

"Always go above and beyond the client's expectations," advises Matt Goodwin of The Cleaning Service Directory. "When you do, your clients will refer your company to their friends and neighbors. That's when you know you are on the right track." Goodwin delivered on this promise by trying to do a small, unexpected service for each client. One of his favorite methods is to move all the furniture in one room and clean under the furniture. All of the items he collects from under the furniture (dog and children's toys, paper clips, pencils, even lost items the homeowner has not seen in years) he puts together with a note for the client telling them where he found their belongings.

> *"Clients were initially shocked that I went that extra mile, but they never forgot it. If you are lucky enough to find an item they know they have lost but cannot locate, they will tell everyone what you did to find it. There is no better advertising than word of mouth!"*

Networking

Networking is similar to word-of-mouth advertising in that it relies on your business being shared with others who might be interested in signing up for your services. The difference is that instead of individual clients doing the referral work, other businesses are spreading the word. For example, Michelle Burnett of You Name It! Home Rescue, LLC, discovered that real estate agents were a valuable source for referring her home cleaning and repairing service to prospective clients. "The most successful marketing strategy for us has been joining a local business networking association," says Burnett. "We were fortunate enough to have a realtor recommend us to **www.angieslist.com**, and that has led to growth."

Networking is free, but earning your place as a service provider in a network takes time. You have to establish that your business offers a quality service. Your placement is a direct result of your ability to provide customers with satisfactory service.

A service provider network may already exist in your area — ask around to other business owners to see if there is one you can join or share information with. If not, establish your own.

To launch your own service provider network, contact other small business owners who might have clients interested in signing up or utilizing cleaning services. Examples are:

✓   Pet sitters

✓   Day care/child care providers

✓   Lawn care companies

✓   Interior decorators

✓   Moving companies

✓   Hospice or health care services

✓   Party or event planners

In your initial contact, tell the service provider about yourself, your company, your service area, the availability of your schedule and a sample of your rates and services. Ask for the same details from them regarding their company, and ask for any type of company literature, such as business cards or flyers, you can pass on to your clients who might be interested in their services.

Keep a file on providers in your network, including their contact information and business details. Tell the other providers that if you receive an inquiry about other business services in your area (such as a client looking for moving company estimates) you will refer the client to them, and ask if they would please do the same for you. Making a customer's life easier will build their trust in you and the other providers, and shows the companies in your network that you are a responsible, reliable service provider.

Community Outreach

Getting involved in your community through community actions is an excellent way to showcase your business and show the people around you that your business cares. Small monetary donations to community organizations in the name of your business are one way to do this. You get the chance to support a cause you believe in and boost your business image at the same time; you can even take the donation as a tax deduction.

There are plenty of other ways to get involved. Donate your services to local organizations who could use a helping hand:

- ✓ Shelters (women's, homeless, church, emergency, animal)

- ✓ Nursing homes

- ✓ Libraries

- ✓ Hospices

✓   Other non-profit organizations

✓   Small volunteer organizations

You may also want to consider donating services to the fund-raising efforts of a particular organization. For example, if a local business is hosting a raffle and donating the proceeds to a worthy cause, you can donate an hour's worth of cleaning or other service to the raffle. Again, any services you donate can be tax-deductible.

Community events and activities may ask you to sponsor them. Local schools routinely list business names in programs, on a board in a gymnasium, or a banner on a baseball field. This will be seen by exactly the type of person your service targets: busy parents who need an extra hand. The same holds true for other events that happen in your community: food drives, car washes, blood donations, recycling initiatives, and similar events. See if there is a place where donors are recognized, such as a newsletter or advertisement in a local paper, and be sure your company is included.

Call and donate a small monetary amount the local television and/or radio stations during their next pledge drive. They may announce donors on air, giving your advertising efforts an extra boost.

Organize a service event with other providers in your network. Choose a worthy activity, such as beautifying a local park or collecting goods for a needy organization. Contact the local media to do a story on your joint efforts.

Trade Shows

The beauty of trade shows is they help businesses in a multitude of ways. Not only do they display your business to the public and to other companies who might need your services, they also offer you a chance to learn more about the industry, new ideas, products and services, and bring you in contact with other business owners with whom you can connect.

Exhibiting your services at a trade show helps market your services to a segment of the population who are seeking to improve their homes and lives. The fees associated with trade shows may be reasonable. Trade shows are held at least once a year. They bring an interested audience directly to your door.

There are two categories of trade shows.

1. **Consumer trade shows** center around home, garden, hobbies, and other types of themes that appeal to a broad variety of potential clients.

2. **Business trade shows** are geared toward businesses marketing their products, equipment, and services to other businesses.

Both types of trade shows can help grow and expand your business. Consider what they have to offer and selectively attend trade shows for specific purposes.

Finding trade shows in your area is easy. Contact your local Chamber of Commerce or convention/exhibition centers where trade shows are held. They can give you a calendar or listing of upcoming events. Check out publications and Web sites centered on trade shows, such as *Trade Show Week*'s Show Directory or the Trade Show News Network at **www.tsnn. com**. You should also ask vendors with whom you have established a relationship about upcoming shows.

Before you sign up to exhibit at a trade show, contact the trade show sponsor to find out specific information on the show. Is it a consumer or business show? What demographic and geographic areas are attending? Can you make direct sales or only collect referrals? What is the expected/anticipated attendance?

Before the show, think about the type of display you will use to highlight your business. Get the measurements of your space in advance to plan appropriately. Keep your display area/booth clean and clutter-free; you are selling cleaning services and want your surroundings to reflect that. Create simple, professional signs that include your basic company information. Include a line or two about how your service can help improve a customer's life.

Take plenty of brochures, business cards, and other promotional materials to the show to pass out to interested visitors. These folks are here for a reason: they are shopping for a service they want and need. Do your best in a positive, non-pressured manner to make a sale or at least collect a sales lead.

One of the best ways to collect sales leads from possible clients is to have a contest in your booth that requires attendees to fill out a registration form collecting their contact information for you to use to get in touch with them after the show. You will want to offer a substantial prize — perhaps a free housecleaning or three rooms of carpet and floors cleaned. Tailor your form to meet the needs of the group attending the show. For example, at a consumer show you should ask questions focused on homeowners, and at a business show you should ask for information on whether or not the company currently has janitorial services. See Appendix B for two sample forms (Business Trade Show Sales Lead and Consumer Trade Show Sales Lead) you can customize.

Giveaways are good to use as a promotional tool as well. Mugs, mouse pads, and pens with your logo, company name, and phone number remind potential clients to get in touch with you if they need your services. Avoid keeping these items out in the open for anyone to take; instead, keep them hidden and share them with those who show a genuine interest in your company. You could also consider distributing coupons to possible customers to give them an extra incentive to follow up with you after the trade show.

Keep your trade show booth lit and open. Avoid placing a table, display material or other bulky items near the open end where customers pass by. You may unwittingly create a block to discourage them from interacting with you. Plan in advance who will cover the booth when you need to leave or take a break. Trade shows are exhausting — you will be on your feet almost the entire day; staying fresh for visitors is important. Put your best face forward for new clients. Leaving your booth unattended for even a moment's time may make a client question your availability and might even invite strangers in a busy convention center to mess with with your equipment or belongings.

The day after the trade show — or as soon as you can — send a follow-up letter or make a call to all of the leads you gathered. Thank them for visiting, include information about your services, and invite them to contact you for any questions or needs they may have. Qualified leads who attend a trade show collect a pile of information from all the vendors and rarely go through each piece after they return home. Remind them of the reasons they found your business so appealing. Give your business the advantage of making a personal contact to show clients what they can expect from your company if they choose your service.

Electronic Advertising

Using the Internet to create a business presence should be a foundation of your marketing strategy. As access to the World Wide Web becomes more affordable and widespread, reaching new clients is as easy as posting your company's information. This may soon be more effective than traditional advertising methods.

The Internet

Putting together a Web site for your business is not expensive (domain names and simple web hosting packages can cost less than $100 per year) or difficult (internet service providers, or ISP's, offer tools to help create content and layout options for your page). It does, however, require time and attention to detail in the beginning. With the tools your ISP provides, you may be able to have a page up and running in a matter of days.

In today's consumer-driven business world, potential clients may perform an initial search for goods and services online via search engines before they look elsewhere. If the customer is taking the time to find your company online and can send you a question via e-mail with the click of a mouse without having to pick up a phone, and if your Web page answers their questions up front, you have the advantage of giving them attention and answers before anyone else has a chance.

Domain Names and Web Hosting Services

To get started, you will first need to register your business name as a web address. Using a common search engine such as **www.google.com**, **www.yahoo.com**, **www.msn.com**, or **www.dogpile.com**, do a search for domain name or domain registration.

This should return a list of links to domain registration sites. These may include:

- ✓ **www.GoDaddy.com**

- ✓ **www.Register.com**

- ✓ **www.NetworkSolutions.com**

You will get thousands of options. Check them out before choosing one.

Do not select on price alone; make sure the company has a good customer service option and other helpful tools. You may have to play around with different formats of your business name to come up with one that is not already in use. Think carefully about this — the simpler the name, the easier it is for customers to recall it. For example, if your name is "Sunshine Cleaners of Howard, Ohio," you might consider shortening the name to "SunshineCleaning.com" or "SunshineCleaningOhio.com."

After you have registered your name, you will need to find a company to host your Web site. Do a search for internet hosting or domain hosts. The results may include:

- ✓ **www.rackspace.com**

- ✓ **http://smallbusiness.yahoo.com/webhosting**

- ✓ **www.1and1.com**

- ✓ **www.GoDaddy.com**

Do your research to find a handful that meet your needs. You will need to host three to five pages, which you may be able to do with the least expensive hosting package available.

Domain registries may also have a number of packages, plans, special offers, and discounts for adding additional services to a basic package. These companies have the ability to not only register your name, but host your site as well. You can choose to host your site at the same place you register your name, or you can opt to have your pages hosted by a company that specializes in hosting. Keeping the two together may be more cost-efficient than having two separate companies. Read the fine print of all contracts before signing. To help compare prices, packages and offers, see the Domain Name Worksheet and Web Host Worksheet in Appendix B.

You will find options to create pages for free — your ISP may provide space for a free Web page or two. However, as tempting as it may be to make a free page with other non-ISPs, be wary of choosing to host your business's Web site on a free host. Free web page providers, such as **www.Bravenet. com**, **www.Geocities.com**, and **www.Tripod.Lycos.com**, come with pop-up advertisements that appear to all customers. Pop-ups are banners, perhaps with blinking lights and flashing boxes that proclaim visitors have won something for free (which they have not), that serious customers find annoying. These pop-ups are a distraction to those viewing your site, and they also turn customers away because they make your company appear less than professional.

Web Page Design

Your Web pages should be clean, uncluttered, informative, professional, and easy to navigate. You can keep the necessary information on your site to five pages or less. Information you will want to feature includes:

1. **Home Page.** Your logo, an inviting photo, and simple text should greet visitors when they first come to your site. You should include details about your business: company name, address, phone number, area served, mission statement, and overview of services. You will also want links to your other pages. It is a good idea to have one common navigation bar located in the same place on every page to help guide visitors to the information they are looking for.

2. **Services and Fees Page.** You may opt not to include all of your fees here; you can say something to the effect of "dependent on the size of area." You will want to include a listing of all the services you offer so that clients can determine whether you have what they need before they proceed further.

3. **Frequently Asked Questions (FAQ).** These are just what they say: a listing of common questions that may be asked of you by potential clients. Develop a thorough FAQ section to show clients you are serious about giving them what they need.

4. **Photo Gallery/Comment Section.** When you finish a job, ask the client to give you a recommendation, feedback, or positive statement about the work you have performed. Take before and after photos of particularly difficult jobs — get the permission of the owner before posting them on your Web site — so interested clients can get a sense for the quality of your work. If you have clients complete a feedback form or evaluation, use quotes and phrases from that as well.

5. **Contact Information.** You may have already listed your business information on your home page, but on your contact page, make the information more personal and specific. Customers want to feel as though you care about them as person, not just a client, so give them the chance to contact your business to speak directly with a person. You can create an e-mail form that will go directly to your e-mail in-box, or you can list the numbers and names of customer service specialists in your company. Even if this is only you, list your name and number as "Contact Patricia at xxx-xxxx for a free estimate." Knowing a person will be there to validate their questions will eliminate hesitation about contacting an unfamiliar business.

How to Use the Internet to Advertise, Promote and Market Your Business or Web site With Little Or No Money from Atlantic Publishing can give you more ideas and guidance on creating a Web presence for your company.

Designing Your Marketing Pieces

Just because you have access to a computer and are comfortable working with word processing programs, you may not have the graphic skills to create a logo or stationery that will grab the interest of potential customers. You want customers to remember your logo and to find it appealing, making them more likely to think of it when they are seeking cleaning services. To make sure this happens, consider using the services of a graphic artist or someone with graphic design skills.

Using a professional graphic designer does not necessarily require a large amount of money; you can advertise at a local community college or even swap services with a local graphic design business to get a logo. Of course, you can use the clip art that comes with word processing or graphic computer programs to create something you like, but people who work with graphic design have the knowledge to help you create more than a picture on paper. They can help you create an image that reflects all that you and your business offer to customers.

Ongoing Advertising Efforts

Consider the calendar when planning advertising. Clients may seek cleaning services when the weather changes or around major holidays when they expect to host and entertain friends and family. Take advantage of these times to target your advertising efforts toward what you think clients will want. For example, offer promotional services and an introductory discount for spring cleaning or a coupon offer in October in anticipation of Thanksgiving and Christmas cleanings.

After you have an established client base and all the customers you can service, resist the urge to cut back on advertising. You want to keep your name on the minds of all potential future clients so that when they see the need you will be the first person they call.

Keep your business message consistent across all media you use in advertising. Tout the value of your business without making unrealistic promises.

Case Study: Matt Goodwin

The Cleaning Service Directory

Pittsfield, NH

www.House-Cleaning-Services.com

Matt Goodwin, Owner

In establishing his cleaning business, advertising in the right places was an important lesson Matt Goodwin learned the hard way.

Radio and television advertising did not bring in the clients Goodwin had hoped it would. He realized he did not have enough revenue or time to remain committed to advertising in these venues. As a result, he discovered what worked best for him was Internet advertising.

His clients were too busy to spend time cleaning and were frequently away from home, perhaps in another city on business. Since they had access to a computer, it made sense to target advertising to these clients so they could research cleaners in their own time. Goodwin's attention to his client's needs paid off. Not only did he build the profits for his own business via Internet advertising, he eventually branched out to offer advertising services for other cleaning services around the world.

Goodwin's advice to new cleaning business owners is to make sure you instill confidence in your cleaning abilities with your clients. Having a professional looking Web site does this, and it gives your business a trustworthy image.

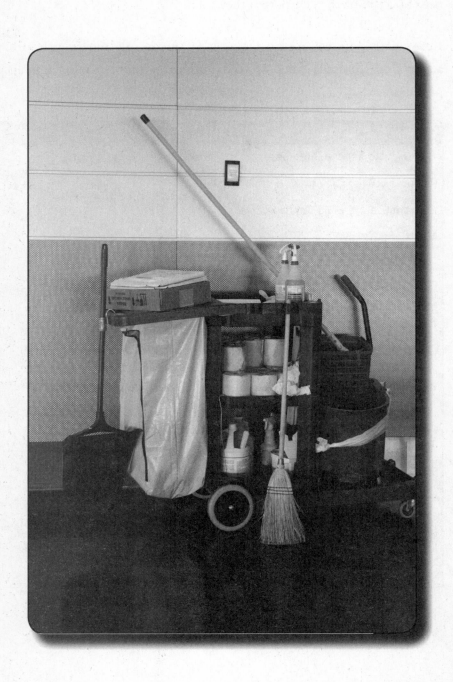

Clients: The Heart of Your Business

Your clients will come to you for the same fundamental reason: they want a clean house, office, or warehouse, but the clients themselves are all unique. Anyone who can afford and is willing to pay your fees, regardless of how frequently they want your services or which combination of services they want, is a client and should be treated with respect and courtesy. Even if you choose not to work with a possible client following the initial consultation, or if they determine your services do not fit into their budget, it is important to present your business in the best possible light to leave them with a positive impression of your company. Even one burned bridge can cause untold trouble in the future, so play it safe and give everyone consideration to make a positive name for yourself.

Case Study: Dan Johnson

Enviro Stat Professional Cleaning Service

Crossville, TN

http://envirostat.net

Dan Johnson, Owner

For Enviro Stat owner Dan Johnson, the third time in the business was the charm. Taking a long, difficult path to owning a multi-service cleaning company, Johnson holds firm to the belief that respect to customers, clients, and the competition is the key to success. Showing clients that you respect them, their homes, and the business they give you comes down to the attention you put into each service provided to customers.

Using corner guards to protect trim when pulling carpet-cleaning hoses into a client's home is one detail that can set your business apart. Wearing simple, clean uniforms, hiring well-groomed, pleasant employees, and having workers wear booties while servicing clients are others.

It is just as important to extend respect to employees. By treating employees the way you like to be treated, such as giving unexpected bonuses on occasion or allowing employees a day or two off now and then makes them more inclined to do their best job.

Go the extra mile by encouraging or requiring employees to respect their competitors as well. Instead of agreeing with clients who complain about a competitor's service, fees, hours of operation, or service crews, teach them to turn the conversation toward highlighting your business. Remember that negativity levied against competitors will filter back to your own business.

"Do your best to be your best" is more than a mission statement for Enviro Stat. It is the core belief of their company.

First Impressions: Meeting Prospective Clients

Even if you are a one-person cleaning operation, conducting yourself in a professional business manner will set you apart from others and leave potential clients with a good feeling. Not only is your business built on your ability to provide customers with a quality service, but a large part of your success is determined by your client's perception of you as a professional. Making a memorable first impression is absolutely crucial to your business growth.

On The Phone

When you first get started, answering client calls may be a bit unnerving. With practice, taking calls as a business owner will become second nature so you will not be as nervous. When starting out, answer your phone with a friendly, open tone and a standard greeting such as, "Thank you for calling Nate's Cleaning Service. How can I help you?" If answering the phone makes you unusually nervous, write your greeting on a card and prop it beside your phone for easy reference. Practice if you need to — stuttering is unprofessional, even if you are caught off guard.

Be pleasant, patient, and knowledgeable. Folks calling you may be as nervous as you are, with little or no experience in knowing what to expect from a cleaning service. They are calling you because you are the expert. Do not give them any reason to think otherwise.

The first questions about your company may center on your rates and the services you offer. One good way to answer this question in advance is to create a company service guide. After you create your service guide, you can post it on your Web page so customers have crucial information before calling you. You can also mail your guide to potential clients who show an interest in your services and would like to do additional research on your company before following up with you in person.

Be prepared to share basic services and pricing information with callers, but do not quote prices yet. That will come with your consultation visit. You will also want to share your payment policies and types of payment you accept, which you determined in Chapter 5.

Take this opportunity to gather necessary information from the potential customer that will help you best determine what they need from your company. "Listening to clients from the first point of contact, which is usually on the phone, is the most important aspect of providing outstanding customer service," says Aileen Johnston, owner of Cinderella Housekeeping Services in Columbus, Ohio. "Find out as many of their expectations as possible to give them what they want. Take any concerns seriously — do not brush them off. They are calling you for a service. Be polite and friendly to make a difference."

A Residential Client Information Form and Commercial Client Information Form are included in Appendix B. Make copies of theses forms and have them near your phone for easy reference. Getting information about the square footage of the home or business area the client wants cleaned, the area of town where they reside to make sure that you serve that area, the services the customer is interested in, the number of rooms, if pets will be present, and an idea of how frequently they would like to schedule your services (daily, nightly, weekly, biweekly, monthly, seasonal) is important. Only with all of this information can you get a sense of whether you can serve them.

You will need to decide whether you want to give estimates over the phone. While giving phone estimates saves you travel time and gives customers instant information, industry professionals discourage this practice. Because you have not seen the space you will be cleaning, you will not have a good sense for the actual size, depth, and time required to complete the job. The client may collect figurines or other memorabilia that require more time and effort to dust or clean properly. The house may be extremely dirty or even a hazardous environment to your workers. There may be stains, spots, or particular areas that need targeted attention because of pets or children.

Resist the urge and occasional pressure to give an estimate without having seen the specific space itself. Your business is based on the quality of services you provide, not the cheapest price in town. You need to be certain you can deliver what you promise to your customers to guarantee your continued success.

Instead of a quote, work with the client to set up a time for you to visit the location they want cleaned to give them an in-depth assessment and estimate. If they are not sure they want you to visit, offer to send them a copy of your service guide (or direct them to your Web site), and ask if you can call them back another day get their phone number so that you can follow up.

In Person

In the cleaning industry, tasks can be done and re-done until they meet a customer's standards, but there is one thing you must do your best the first time, every time — making a first impression when meeting a client.

Everyone is judged when we meet someone new. There is no way to avoid this; it is simply human nature. Use it to your advantage by presenting yourself as a competent business owner from the start. Otherwise you will not be seen or treated as a professional.

For client meetings, blue jeans are inappropriate unless you are performing a service at the time you meet with the client. Fancy clothes are not necessary, but you do need to appear professional. Your cleaning uniform shirt with a blazer or jacket and clean pair of dress pants qualifies as a standard outfit. Comfortable, clean shoes are important as you will be on your feet during the estimate process, working from one room to another room to room with your client. Give your client the chance to focus on your message and your services, not your appearance.

A firm handshake, consistent eye contact, and a smile show respect and confidence. If you are a smoker, do not smoke before meeting a client. You are selling the promise of clean and fresh, and the smell of cigarette smoke is neither. Clients may be put off by even the slightest odor of smoke from your clothes, so be careful.

Other business etiquette to consider when meeting new or potential clients:

- ✓ **Manners**. Please and thank you are two small words that leave a big impression.

- ✓ **Return calls and inquiries promptly**. Clients are calling because they are interested in services now. The longer you wait to get back with them, the bigger chance they will call someone else who can meet their needs sooner.

- ✓ **Show a personal interest in the client and their spaces**. Though cleaning is a business, give clients your undivided attention by noticing photos of their grandchildren or collection of antique spoons. This shows your attention to detail and that you value them as individuals, not just clients.

- ✓ **Professionalism above all**. Resist the temptation to gossip about competitors, even if the client steers the conversation in that direction. If clients share criticism of other cleaners, use it as a learning experience. Do not argue, even if you are right. Do not discuss personal relationships or share off-color jokes, even if your client is a close friend. Conduct yourself with dignity.

The Value of a Walkthrough

From short tour of a potential client's home, you can ascertain a wealth of information that will be helpful to you in preparing your cleaning crews for servicing the customer's home or business that you could not gather from a phone conversation. Not only will you learn the layout and condition of the home/business's physical space, you will also learn whether they will be a good client or one you will need to work with.

Service Estimates

One of the main purposes of conducting a walkthrough at the customer's home is to get a sense of the way rooms are arranged, how much work it will take to complete the jobs they request, and the amount of time and size of the work force you will need to dedicate to doing a thorough job.

Before heading out to give an estimate, be sure to let someone know where you are going, especially if it is in an unfamiliar part of town or new neighborhood. Put together a small tote bag or other carrying case that contains the tools you may need: pencils, pens, a copy of your customer service guide, business cards, a Residential Quote Form and/or a Janitorial Estimate Form (both which can be found in Appendix B), and anything else you need.

When first meeting the client, ask them to give you a tour. Do not just take the initiative to walk through their home and tell them what they need; rather, have them guide you through in the way they are comfortable. They are opening their home to you. Although you hope to build a client relationship with them, you are still a stranger at this point. Treat them with respect to build their comfort level and confidence in your knowledge.

Use your notepad to collect pertinent information about everything in each room that will require the attention of your cleaning crew. One good idea is to label the top of each page with the name of the room so that when you return to draw up the layout of the space for your service plan, you can either staple your observations to the form or list the items you have taken note of on the actual room plan page itself.

Details to note as you walk through a potential home or business:

✓ Evidence of pets, their names, and where the client intends to keep them (caged, closed room, or outside in a locked area) while your employees service the home — Note where pets prefer to spend their time so that your cleaners can pay special attention to those parts of the home.

✓ The knickknacks and collectibles in each room — These will require extra care and time to dust or clean according to client preference. Ask how the client would like you to deal with these things: if they want you to clean them all each time, if they would like a monthly dusting, or if they will take care of cleaning these items themselves. If you have reservations about cleaning a priceless wall hanging or piece of furniture, note that as well. There may be pieces in the room that are out of your area of expertise or comfort level. It is better for you to avoid these than accidentally damage them with well-intentioned but inappropriate cleaning processes. Inquire if there is anything in the room the client prefers you not clean or touch.

✓ If children live in the home, you may request that a client prepare for your visits by putting away toys and games to save your workers time in performing their duties. You can also choose to have toy pickup as part of your basic services, or you can ask clients to prepare for your visits with common courtesy.

✓ Will anyone else be present in the home — You are not obligated to baby-sit or act as guardian for children or adults of any age while you clean. In agreeing to do so, you may be creating an unhealthy, unsafe environment for your employees or yourself. Families may have aging parents or older children living at home with them, and you need to decide if you feel safe with them hanging around while doing your work.

At the conclusion of your walkthrough, you should have enough information to make an estimate on the total cost of the job, the time it will take your employees to complete the tasks and when you can schedule the clients into your rotation for service.

Industry experts are divided on the issue of building in time between the actual estimate and signing the client up for your services. One option is to give clients the information and allow them to sign an agreement for services on the spot, after which you schedule them for an actual cleaning. Another is to share the estimate with the potential customer and allow them a day or two to go over your numbers, make certain you have included all the services they have requested, and be sure they are comfortable with the prices and terms of your agreement before signing a customer agreement form for your services.

If you decide to wait, you need to be the one to contact the customer with a follow-up call. Be punctual and call them when you say you will; beginning a relationship with a late response sends a message to clients that other things are more important to you than their business.

If clients request changes to the original agreement, be prompt in providing them with a new estimate written to their specifications. "When cleaners and customers do not have a clear meeting of the minds, there can be problems. Since we guarantee our work, good communication is essential," says Mona Makela, owner of Heavenly Maid Cleaning Services in Troutdale, Oregon. "To avoid misunderstandings, we came up with a detailed checklist that allows customers to prioritize jobs and cleaners to note when the job was completed. Our customers love this option and it helps increase satisfaction."

Screening Clients

Just as the potential client will learn about you and your company during the walkthrough process, you have an excellent opportunity to discover details about the client that will help you assess how well they fit with your business. Use the walkthrough to your advantage when meeting new customers. What you can learn about them while you are in their home or business gives insight into the type of customer they will be. In the familiar surroundings of their home or business, clients tend to be more relaxed and, as a result, more themselves. They may answer questions more honestly and without hesitation.

As a new business owner, you will need to develop your ability to read and understand all types of people with whom you come into contact: employees, clients, vendors, and other business owners. Getting a good feel for the type of person you are dealing with takes time to master. The walkthrough process is an excellent time to refine this skill.

Dream Clients

Regardless of the size of the job, each client deserves to be respected and valued. Making them feel important is crucial to them spreading the word to others about the value of your service.

Dream clients are those who extend courtesy and respect toward you and your staff each time you meet. They recognize you as a valuable and knowledgeable business owner and defer to your expertise in scheduling crews, estimating jobs, and noting specific circumstances that may affect your crew's ability to complete a job. Dream clients make your crews' jobs as easy as possible by preparing in advance for their arrival. They pay the agreed-upon amount on time and call you immediately with questions or concerns.

Risky Clients

To anticipate which clients may pose problems for you and your employees down the road, trust your gut instincts. If you notice that you are uncomfortable in a home or a business as part of an initial assessment, that feeling of unease or uncertainty is an indication that you need to pay close attention to the person or surroundings. Aside from a negative reaction to a possible customer, there are a variety of skills you can train yourself to look for that may pose potential problems down the line.

Interpersonal Skills

- ✓ Clients who complain or argue over your estimates or anticipated costs

- ✓ Clients who follow your staff and bother them as they attempt to complete their cleaning tasks

- ✓ Clients who are overly demanding or inflexible regarding scheduling

- ✓ Clients who degrade, verbally abuse, or talk down to your staff

- ✓ Clients who do not give positive feedback

- ✓ Clients who make overly-personal, racial, intimate, or sexual jokes

- ✓ Clients who do not understand the limits and abilities of what your service can do for them

- ✓ Clients who cannot afford your services

Physical Signals

Potential issues may be brought to light not by how a person behaves but by the surroundings in which they live or work. Do careful investigation at all possible job sites to be sure you are not sending your crew to do a job which cannot be completed or poses a health or safety threat to their well-being.

Details to note:

- ✓   An appalling or hazardously filthy home or business

- ✓   Any type of unsafe structure, such as unfinished or unsafe stairs, insect or rodent infestation, leaky plumbing, or a layer of trash covering the floor or piled on counters or furniture

- ✓   Unsupervised/unrestrained pets on premises and the client with no plan to remedy the problem, even at your request

- ✓   A physical layout beyond the abilities of your staff and equipment

How to Say No

For the safety of your employees and the reputation of your business, there will be times when you must refuse a job or end a current contract. These are not easy decisions. When you are starting out, getting new clients may be difficult; you may be willing to try a customer despite clues they are not a good fit for your company. Do yourself and your workers a favor and carefully weigh the pros and cons of the decision before signing on a client you have reservations about.

If you find yourself in a situation where a potential client or job is not an

Client Expectations: Developing a Service Manual

One of the best ways to set your business apart from the local competition and to establish your business as a legitimate company is through a service manual for clients. A service manual will boost your professional image and will save time answering questions potential customers ask regarding your services, fees, policies and procedures. It will help sell your services and serve as a guiding document for your business. Refer to it in your advertising, and advise potential clients on how to find it on your Web site.

A service manual is not a one-time deal. You will need to service manual updated it on a regular basis to be sure it reflects current rates, areas serviced, contact information, and other important details. Use it as a printed form of valid information clients can use to select your business instead of another.

You may choose to have the customer print the service manual information from your Web site, or you can print copies and hand them out to potential clients as they contact you. There is no right or wrong way as long as the option is there for the customer.

If you do the printing, present the manual in a folder or a binder. Your manual may be small if you are a one-person cleaning crew, but the material is important for the customer to have for reference. You can even color coordinate the binder/folder and papers inside with the colors of your logo for an additional boost to your professional image.

Sections of a Service Manual

Your service manual does not have to be lengthy to be effective. Brief and informative is actually a better choice as customers do not have time to wade through unnecessary details. Appendix B includes a detailed outline to guide you in creating your own service manual.

Cover Page and Table of Contents

The rule of thumb for a cover page is: clean and simple. Title and number each page. Always include a cover page. Center your logo on the cover page, and, in bold letters above or below, center your business name in a large font.

When arranging your cover page, include the following pertinent information:

- ✓ Complete business name

- ✓ Your name

- ✓ Mailing address

- ✓ E-mail address

- ✓ Web site address

- ✓ Contact numbers — phone, cell, pager, fax

- ✓ Services offered —one or two lines about the types of services you offer

- ✓ Service area — one or two lines of the geographic area your business serves

A table of contents is optional. If you have a variety of specialty services or janitorial options, for example, you can define these services on the table of contents to help customers easily find information.

Mission and Vision Statements

Here is where you share with customers the mission and vision statement you created as part of your business plan. You can include one or both. Since your mission statement is your action statement, it is wise to include it. If your table of contents or cover page is not cluttered, you may choose to include your vision and/or mission statements there as well.

Consultation Process

Creating a written version of your consultation process is as much for you and your employees as it is for customers. If a potential client downloads your service manual before speaking with you, it gives them a clear picture of how your consultation process works.

Briefly explain the steps in the process beginning with the initial customer contact. Include the normal length of the process and walkthrough, what the customer can expect at the consultation, and what information they will need to know to prepare for your meeting.

Services Offered and Base Rates

The services offered and base rates section is where you will delineate exactly what you will and will not be able to do for them. If you offer a wide variety of services, do not worry that this section might be a large one. It may take ten to twenty pages to detail your services. Your goal is to give customers explicit details on what to expect from your company when they hire you. Potential clients will have questions you have not yet considered, so be as detailed as you can to help them understand the important facts up front.

The easiest way to describe your services is to name the service in a sentence or in one line and then define the service in a short paragraph. Complex services may require additional paragraphs.

You may also want to include a list of services you do not perform for clients. In addition to listing your services, you can include the basic rate for each service one. Of course your actual rates will vary based on the job site and size, but it is helpful to give clients an idea of where your prices start so that if you are too expensive for their budget, neither of you wastes time on a consultation.

Another consideration for this section is to mention the optional services you provide. Since these are in addition to your regular services, you can skip listing a fee and say "fee available upon consultation" to make customers aware that you offer the services and that they can inquire about them.

Company Policies

Before a customer signs a contract, they need to be made aware of the policies and procedures that govern your business. In this section, clearly spell out details of expected behavior on these issues:

- ✓ Cancellation procedures — How soon before a service a client can cancel without penalty, the penalty rate for rescheduling, how to contact you, and how to reschedule

- ✓ How you will handle employees arriving to the customer's home or office for a job and being unable to service the client on time

- ✓ How you will handle employees arriving late because of traffic or weather delays

- ✓ Whether you or the client will provide equipment or cleaning products

- ✓ Expectations for employee/client interaction

- ✓ Who to contact with service questions, comments, or complaints

Scheduling Services

Clients need to know how to contact you when they want your services.

They will need to understand how you set the schedule and the time you or your crew plan to arrive. Consider these questions when writing the section regarding scheduling services:

✓ **When you schedule services, will you give a reminder call?** — With regular customers, find out if they want to contact you each time they need service, or if they want you to schedule them in advance.

✓ **Who do they contact for scheduling services?** — Make sure clients understand your deadlines for requesting/scheduling services. For example, if they need a cleaning the next week, do they need to request service by noon on Sunday. If the customer cancels, you will want to let them know how soon can they expect your crew to reschedule.

Safety and Security

Clients will want to know how you will be storing their keys and access information before giving permission to proceed. Put them at ease by detailing your security process for customer keys.

One way to secure our clients' keys is with a coding system. Create a unique code for each client, and use that code only when referring to a client on documentation instead of listing identifying personal information. You or trusted crew chiefs should be the only people with access to this information.

Your code can be a color, number, or combination system. You can color-code by type of services the clients request (residential, janitorial, daily, weekly, biweekly, monthly, or seasonal) or the day of the week they receive service. You may, for example, keep all Tuesday keys together on a key ring in order of the time the client receives service during the day.

Customer information, keys, and identification codes should all be stored in separate locations. Keys should be stored in a safe when not in use by a cleaning crew. When you receive keys from clients, code them immediately, and at the en d of a cleaning contract, have clients sign to verify that you have returned their keys. Failure to do so could result in legal issues if something occurs at the customer's home — even if you and your employees are not responsible. Require your employees to sign out keys daily and return them to your safe each day. Do not include any type of identifying information with the keys that might help a stranger locate that customer, such as name, address, or phone number.

You will also want to assure clients that none of their personal information will be shared with anyone outside your company. You will find that as an established business, other businesses may request your client information for marketing purposes. These companies may be willing to pay cash for customer information, but the price for selling customer information is a loss of business integrity and trustworthiness, so resist the urge.

Safety is an important element of your business. Include your policy on employee safety in this section as well. You will want to develop that covers the following areas:

✓   Whether your workers will work with other contractors or service providers present (roofers, plumbers, carpenters, or other service personnel). Cleaning services do not normally do this because they are cleaning for the client, not the service provider. If a contractor clutters a room your crews have cleaned, you will need to do it again at your own expense. Save yourself and your employees the aggravation by establishing this policy.

✓   If visitors will be in the house at the same time as your crews, require your clients to notify you so you can make your workers aware of this.

✓   If your clients are aware of anything that may compromise the health or safety of your workers, require them to notify you. For example, if a door is loose, if a portion of flooring or a wall is damaged, or if an area needing cleaning is structurally unsafe.

You may also want to include information for the client if they are interested in verifying your insurance and bonding information. You can list your insurance company and the name and contact information of your agent for clients to inquire about your insurance.

Billing and Payment Policies

In this section you will spell out your expectations for customers regarding billing and payment. Details to include:

✓   Payment terms (before, after, within 30 days, left at the residence, or mailed)

✓   Payment types (cash, credit, check)

✓   If you require a deposit fee for new clients

✓   Late payment fees

✓   Billing cycle details (weekly, monthly, biweekly)

✓   If you bill, how customers will receive the bill (mail, e-mail, left in a specific place in the home or business)

✓   How you will handle receipts

Contract Renewal and Terms of Agreement

The information in this section should be straightforward. Consider:

✓ What length is your standard contract?

✓ How long do customers have to make changes to their service agreement, by either removing services or adding options?

✓ If you terminate a client's services, what is the procedure?

✓ If clients terminate services with you, what is the procedure?

10

Setting Fees

Setting your fees — the prices you will charge for services you offer to clients — can be an unnerving part of getting your business established. You do not want to price your fees too low and wind up exhausted at the end of your day with little profit to show for it. Likewise, if you overprice your services, clients may be unwilling to pay or budget for your services.

Choosing the right fees, based on a number of independent factors, is a tough job. It is a job you should not take lightly. You may discover after setting your initial prices that you need to reconsider and adjust them based on market demand, your success or lack of business, or in response to local changes in the cleaning service industry. Do not let this intimidate you. Use the opportunity to adjust prices to benefit your company. A reasonable, fair price for the quality of your services is the best guarantee for future profits.

Considerations Before Setting Your Fees

A number of elements need to be addressed before you can present the public with your actual fees. If you are not comfortable with numbers, pricing your services can be one of the least enjoyable activities in establishing your business. Resist the impulse to make quick, hurried decisions; doing so will either result in lower profits or put your fees in an unreasonable range. Your main competition is not other businesses but clients who believe they can do the same job themselves for less.

Do not be afraid to make mistakes in the pricing process, as there is a learning curve. You may find that as your skills improve and you become more efficient in performing your cleaning jobs, you can increase profits by changing from one type of fee structure to another — from an hourly fee to a per-job fee, for example.

Consider the value and quality of your services as the main factor in what should drive your rates, not your actual time spent. If you choose to set your rates low to convince clients to try your services, you have difficulty making enough money to hire adequate staff, and clients may be reluctant to hire you thinking your low fees reflect a lack of professional experience.

Case Study: Darryl C. Reed

Crystal Crystal Carpet Care

Columbus, OH

www.crystalcrystalcarpet.com

Darryl C. Reed, Owner

When starting your business, do not cave in to the pressure of setting your prices lower than the market average in your area to entice clients. You will cause yourself problems that may be difficult or even impossible to solve.

Commercial and janitorial services are commodities where the lowest acceptable market prices are pretty well set. If a new business owner comes in and believes they can go lower to sign additional jobs or contracts, they had better have something innovative and unique as far as cleaning services that no one else knows about. Pricing your services unusually low is equal to buying a job, not developing a business. Of course, if your business'es mission statement is to get

Case Study: Darryl C. Reed

jobs or money, this will work temporarily. It is easy to get jobs when your prices are ridiculously low, but doing business this way will have an effect on the amount of time you can devote to running and creating a name for your business. Setting prices too low just to get accounts has destroyed the lives of more than one cleaning service.

Avoiding this is easy. Take time to understand how to look at your costs. Labor will be the largest factor, then equipment, overhead, and the costs of the sale. Find out what the costs will be to perform the service, apply your profit percentage to that, then look at the market to see where folks are pricing their services. You will discover that there are indeed companies who set their prices deliberately low or believe they truly have a new way of doing things, but they will not last or they will not be able to establish their business because their prices are not compatible with making a profit. Be sure there are enough profits to grow your business, not just do the job. Consider what is good business for you and your company and stick with jobs that will only enhance your company goals. Someone else will do the rest!

How to Set Your Fees

Understand your actual business expenses. This includes everything from supplies and equipment to insurance, licensing, and other expenditures. Keep an expense record sheet (a sample biannual expense record sheet can be found in Appendix B) to record as many actual expenses as possible in the initial months of your business. Use real data whenever possible, and use educated estimates on the rest. The more authentic figures you have, the more accurate your end figures will be, and they will hold more meaning for the needs of your business.

One method for getting a handle on the going rates of cleaning services in your area is performing your own research. Make a list of every cleaning service in your target market by using the Yellow Pages, online searches, newspapers, and other advertisements. Dedicate time to researching the fees of these businesses. A day of or two should be adequate to gather what you will need.

After you gather the contact information for these companies, enter it into a database or use index cards to create a separate listing for each business as a place to record their responses to your questions. Questions for comparison include:

- ✓ What is their geographic service area?

- ✓ Would they travel outside that area for a fee?

- ✓ Are they insured, licensed, and bonded? Reputable businesses may be willing to share their insurance information with potential customers.

- ✓ How do they charge for services? (per job, per hour)

- ✓ What are their basic rates?

- ✓ Do they require a minimum number of hours per job?

- ✓ How long have they been in the cleaning business?

- ✓ How soon could they visit for an estimate?

- ✓ What are their payment options and terms?

- ✓ Do they have a service manual or frequently asked questions document?

✓ How many employees do they have?

Contact these businesses and inquire about their services as if you were a potential customer — without tipping them off that you are researching for your company. You can question these businesses about their rates and services as long as you do not deliberately use that information to set your prices low and steal their clients. This is an unethical practice called undercutting. You may find owners hesitant to share information if they have reason to believe you are anything other than a potential client, so be respectful and responsible if they choose not to answer. You cannot and should not force an answer. If a provider insists on an in-house estimate, politely decline or mention that you need to check your schedule and will get back to them.

Three Major Factors in Setting Fees

There are three important financial components to be addressed in-depth to determine the rates best for your services: labor, materials, and equipment; overhead operating cost; and profit margin.

Labor, Materials, and Equipment

You will need to estimate labor, materials, and equipment in the beginning stages of your business. After you have success in completing jobs and earning profit, you can use these records to guide your future figures.

Labor costs are the sum of wages, benefits, and other monetary compensation you offer employees. Do not forget to include yourself and your labor contribution to any job you perform. Judge your labor costs on the percentage of work you put into a job rather than the straight amount of time it takes you to finish.

Labor rates are normally calculated per hour, while equipment and materials can be expressed as a weekly, monthly or quarterly figure.

Overhead Operating Cost

Overhead operating cost is a group of expenses necessary to the continued functioning of your business that do not directly generate profits and are not labor or materials. Specifically, overhead includes expenditures for advertising, accounting, indirect labor, insurance, legal fees, rent/mortgage, office supplies, taxes, travel, telephone, and utilities.

Your overhead rate is figured as a percentage of your labor and equipment costs. Initially, you will not have past operating expenses for reference, so using industry-average figures for this purpose is a standard practice. Do not blindly continue to operate with these numbers, however. As your business grows, adjust the overhead rate to reflect the actual numbers of your business.

After operating for a year, you can recalculate your overhead based on your prior year actual figures. Total a year's worth of expenses (not including labor and equipment), then divide the sum by your total cost of labor and equipment. The result is your overhead rate, which we will use in the pricing formula.

Profit Margin

Making a profit from your services relies on the difference between two things: how much it costs for you to provide a service and what you charge the client for performing that service. Determine your net profit, or how much you plan to make on a job, by applying a markup percentage to the amount you estimate to clients. Your estimate should reflect the total costs of labor, equipment, and overhead for the work you complete.

To bring in the profits you seek, you will need to add a markup percentage, either in dollars or in a percentage to your actual cost of services, to the actual cost of your services. For more advice on calculating markup percentages, see the Calculating Markup worksheet in Appendix B.

Pricing Your Services

Three basic pricing strategies will normally cover the types of work you will perform: per hour, per job or service, and per type of service.

Per Hour Price Rates

When estimating large cleaning jobs that are difficult to classify in terms of actual time they will require to complete, per-hour rates are common. This is also the easiest way for new business owners to set prices as they work toward making services more efficient. Other jobs for which an hourly fee is appropriate include:

- ✓ Seasonal services

- ✓ Jobs that require hourly paid staff

- ✓ Unfamiliar jobs or jobs where you do not have time on the premises to evaluate the job before performing services

- ✓ Basic housecleaning

Per Job or Per Service Rates

Charging clients per job or per service you perform requires additional knowledge about the actual cost, overhead, markup, and profit involved. Jobs where you have the exact same working environment with little variation may be appropriately charged per service. These might include:

✓ Post-move apartments or condominiums

✓ Common area cleanings in apartments or large buildings

✓ Post-construction new home builds

✓ Model home cleanings

✓ Pet sitting and cleanup services

✓ Specialty jobs requested by client for which require additional staff/pay

✓ Select janitorial jobs after the first cleaning

✓ Select home cleaning jobs after the first cleaning

Per Type of Service Rates

Residential Service Fees

Residential and maid services may charge per-hour until a cleaning pattern for a client is established; it may be a more advantageous use of time to work on a per-job fee.

Commercial/Janitorial Service Fees

Overhead runs more for janitorial services — averaging anywhere from 20 to 50 percent of labor and equipment costs. Industry average net profits for janitorial services are between ten to thirty percent of gross revenue.

Carpet Cleaning Services

Unlike residential and commercial cleaning, carpet cleaners charge per square foot, not hourly or per job. Overhead for carpet cleaning is much higher —

45 to 55 percent of labor and equipment costs. Profits average from 39 to 49 percent from gross revenues.

Estate Cleaning Services

Since estate cleanings are such a large venture, it is acceptable to negotiate these jobs on a commission. You can charge clients a percentage of the estate's final selling price based on the amount of work you determine the project will require. Be sure your agreement is put into a contract between your business and the family, executor, or legal representative of the estate before beginning work. Pay attention to the terms, and be certain to work within them.

11

Roll Up Your Sleeves & Clean

With the foundational business information covered — planning, financing, and everything in between — there are still the practical details of what it takes to deliver the clean your customers expect.

A cleaning business is a service everyone thinks they can do well. At one point or another in their lives, every person has cleaned something; therefore, there are quick assumptions that they can do a better job for less. Remind your customers or potential customers that part of the service you are selling is the time they will save and be able to devote to another part of their busy lives by hiring you. After you show clients, that you do a thorough job for a reasonable fee, they will place a higher value on your services.

In addition to the time you save them, you are also bringing order into their homes and lives and infusing their surroundings with freshness regularly. They will look forward to your visits with a hopeful expectation. When you leave behind quality work that speaks for itself, you can expect customer satisfaction on a multitude of levels.

Organizing and refreshing a customer's home in a set period while on a budget is no small task. This is the main reason for keeping you and your staff adequately trained and up-to-date on the latest cleaning methods and procedures. While every customer account is unique, the tasks you perform in the home or office environment are essentially the same. Knowing the proper way to clean and execute your services guarantee savings in both time and effort, leaving you with additional time for clients.

Case Study: LaVerne Newton & Michael A. Cleveland

Sincerely Chores: Non-Toxic Cleaning For You and Yours

Woodhaven, NY

www.sincerelychores.com

LaVerne Newton and

Michael A. Cleveland, co-owners

Part of the success of any cleaning business is the ability to respond to changes in techniques, customer demands, and other elements in the cleaning industry to meet the needs of clients. To meet the growing interest of clients for non-toxic, or "green" cleaning, Sincerely Chores focused their efforts on developing this niche in their customer base.

Providing services with a specialty focus is not just limited to the cleaning solutions and products Sincerely Chores uses. Clients may not be aware of the harm that harsh cleaning chemicals can cause and are grateful for the time Sincerely Chores takes to educate others and providing environmentally friendly cleaning solutions.

Families with children and pets are especially grateful for these workshops and classes that show the dangers in their homes from chemicals in popular cleaning products. In addition, monthly newsletters feature articles focused on cleaning specific parts of the home and appliances as well as a "to-do" list with advice on what chores should be given special attention during a particular month.

Case Study: LaVerne Newton & Michael A. Cleveland

Sincerely Chores takes green cleaning one step further by providing clients with a clean, healthy environment with their own line of non-toxic cleaning products. This supports their goal to provide a climate free of harmful toxins that is safe for homes, families, and pets.

Fundamental Cleaning Strategies

The jobs you complete for residential clients will differ a bit from those you perform for your janitorial customers. We will address these differences but first we will focus on the fundamental cleaning strategies that apply to nearly every cleaning job.

Whether you are cleaning three rooms or an office complex, these common strategies are universally successful:

✓ Clean from top to bottom, left to right in a circle around the room or space.

✓ Avoid backtracking by carrying as many cleaning supplies and products with you as you can. Every step back wastes time, which wastes money.

✓ When you enter a room, open windows and doors and turn on the lights to gain adequate lighting for the job.

✓ Do all the dry work first then the wet work. Tidy and neatly stack items, dust, polish, dry mop, and vacuum. Then use spray cleaners, give them time to work, wipe down and wet mop.

✓   Set patterns of service for each house and each room. Cleaners recommend cleaning from low to high traffic areas (upstairs to downstairs, bathrooms then bedrooms then family/living rooms, then kitchens).

Residential and Home Cleaning

If you are working alone, you can clean your client spaces in whatever way you choose. Select a method that works for both you and the client to maximize your time on tasks, and go with it. However, if you have crews completing your jobs, there are options to consider in breaking a job down into manageable pieces.

✓   Assign cleaning team members (two to three people per team) to clean only a specific room or area in the home. If a client is dissatisfied with one particular area, the responsible team member is the one with whom you discuss the issue.

✓   If you have two team members, you can organize cleaning chores so that one is responsible for performing the dry chores and the other the wet tasks. These specialties can be swapped weekly to break monotony, or you may discover certain staff members do a particular job well because they enjoy it more, and you may choose to leave them in that job.

In a pair, your crews have equal responsibility for providing service. In groups of three or more, it is a good idea to appoint a crew leader or supervisor familiar with your company and expectations to serve as an accountability person as well as a motivator.

Bedrooms, Living Rooms, and Other Basic "Room" Areas

Dust first, starting with the ceiling behind the door. Using your long-handled duster, do the ceiling/wall, and then move downward to bookshelves, paintings, and furniture. End with tabletops and baseboards.

Apply dusting product to your duster only, never directly to the surface you are dusting. Television screens can be dusted with an electrostatic cloth or with glass cleaner applied directly to a cloth. Swipe electrical switch plates and covers with a cloth dampened with window cleaner.

Vacuum the room by beginning with the corner furthest from the door and vacuum your way out of the room, not into the room to avoid tracking dirt where you have cleaned. Use attachments to get dust from blinds and drapes if this is part of your services. Get into the corners and baseboards with proper vacuum tools.

Bathrooms

If you encounter substantial dust, hair, or dirt on the floors or walls of the bathroom, vacuum first to make sure you do not stir it up as you clean or leave it behind on wet surfaces. Vacuuming throw rugs is unnecessary and time-consuming, so take these outside for a quick, hard shake to get rid of any dirt.

Dust the bathroom from the top down, left to right. Apply all-purpose cleaner to the tub walls from to bottom and allow it to sit before wiping down. If the tub is fiberglass, use a non-abrasive cleaner. Glass shower doors are best cleaned with glass cleaner. Do not forget to check out the tracks of shower doors and clean them with a toothbrush or small brush and paper towel.

Next, clean the toilet with disinfectant. Scrub the bowl with a brush, flush, and wipe down the seat with disinfectant as well. As you disinfect the bowl, wipe down bathroom walls and electrical light plates and switches.

Follow your toilet cleaning with a cleaning of sinks, faucets, and countertops. You should clean the soap dish as well. Clean the mirror last as any splatters of water from the sink will ruin your shine. Spray with glass cleaner and wipe down with lint-free paper towels.

As you leave the bathroom to clean other spaces, vacuum or dry mop your way out, and then wet mop the floor if it is not carpeted.

Kitchen

Pre-treat heavily soiled/dirty areas with degreaser. (All-purpose cleaner is not formulated to clean grease.) Let this set and work while you get started cleaning the kitchen. You may also want to pre-treat the oven with oven cleaner if it is warranted and if it is a part of your services.

Dust cabinet tops and windowsills, then clean windows (if a part of your services) except for those above the sink. Dampen a cleaning cloth with all-purpose cleaner, or save time by dampening several. Make your way around the kitchen, and wipe down countertop appliances (microwave, coffee, toaster/toaster oven, mixer) with the pre-treated cloths. Follow with an application of disinfectant to countertops, cleaning under appliances as well.

Next, clean larger appliances — dishwasher front, refrigerator, oven front, stovetop, washing machine/dryer. Empty trash and clean the exterior of garbage cans. You may choose to clean out the inside of garbage cans for an additional fee.

Last, using a non-abrasive all-purpose or specialty cleaner, depending on the surface, clean the sink and give it a good rinse. Clean the window above the sink. Vacuum or dry mop and wet mop your way out of the kitchen.

Stairways and Hallways

Stairways should be done as you transition from one level to another. Start at the top. Dust stairways and dry mop wooden surfaces. If stairs are carpeted, use a canister vacuum to clean each stair.

A Checklist of Residential Services is included in Appendix B.

Commercial & Janitorial Cleaning

As janitorial jobs are larger jobs to complete, it makes sense that you will need more employees to accomplish the tasks your clients' request.

Like residential cleaning, you will want a supervisor or crew leader to oversee your cleaning teams and the work they do. Choose someone with good interpersonal skills and background cleaning knowledge. You may want to consider individuals who have been with your company for a while and are familiar with your operations. You will also want to pay your supervisors more than your workers. One to two dollars additional per hour is a good average.

Select working teams to reflect group members who get alone well with each other. Bickering and arguments on a cleaning job just wastes time, so plan ahead to minimize or eliminate this. Keep your teams together as much as possible. Changing teams from job to job requires a learning curve and is counterproductive to having employees get to know each other. The longer they are together, the stronger their unity and productivity.

When assigning tasks, the supervisor should share the cleaning tasks with workers. Janitorial work is best divided in terms of wet and dry work. If you discover some of your workers prefer one type to another, try scheduling to reflect that preference. When employees do a job they enjoy, they do it with extra attention to detail, which translates into positive staff morale.

When you select dry and wet crews, each has a different set of expectations.

Dry Jobs

For those on the dry crew, these are important tasks they will need to complete:

- ✓ Remove and empty all garbage cans, bins, and trash receptacles.

- ✓ Pull small furniture (chairs, desks, magazine racks) away from the walls.

- ✓ Using a dry mop or duster with an extension, clean the perimeter of each room or space to be cleaned by dusting ceiling to floor, from left to right. Do not neglect corners or baseboards. Service every wall in this manner, even those outside the general room configuration. Remember to dust windows, windowsills, and behind doors.

- ✓ Follow dusting with a vacuuming of the area. Begin in the corner furthest from you and work back toward yourself to avoid walking on areas you have vacuumed. Get into cracks, crevices, and small spaces.

Wet Jobs

For those on the wet crew, these are important tasks they will need to complete:

✓ Wash or wipe down walls — top to bottom, left to right.

✓ Clean and scrub toilets, shine and polish bathroom surfaces, and clean mirrors.

✓ Scrub other hard surfaces — countertops in break/lunch/copy rooms, for example — and mop your way out of each room as you finish.

With janitorial services, it is not necessary to perform all tasks every day. When you initially contract with clients, discuss what jobs they want, need, and expect you to do daily and what they would like done weekly or monthly.

Maintain a file of information for each client and what services they want. To keep your crews aware of when particular tasks should be performed, put the information into a checklist, and have employees date and initial next to the task after it has been completed. This checklist serves a dual purpose in that you can also use it to verify work done with the customer. A Janitorial Services Checklist is included in Appendix B.

Carpet Cleaning

The techniques used to clean customer carpets will vary by the methods you use and prefer. A wide variety of cleaners (liquid and powder), sanitizers, spotters, deodorizers, concentrates, and stain-resistant treatments exist to help complete your tasks. Knowing the mission of your cleaning job is important in selecting the right products for your purpose.

As you branch out and clean more carpets, you will discover customer dissatisfaction with issues such as drying time and carpets not appearing as clean as clients anticipated. To head this off before it becomes an issue, learn about carpet cleaning yourself so you can offer clients honest, professional information. Require your employees or technicians to complete training satisfactorily before ever servicing a client, and give accurate estimates.

When you visit a home, note the condition of carpet and be upfront with the customer if you believe sections of the carpeting will require extra time or attention due to poor condition or overly-soiled pile. Let clients know in advance of writing an estimate as a professional courtesy, and avoid underestimating for the sake of getting a job. You will want to list the date of the estimate, the job date, time, and address/location, as well as the tasks agreed upon by you and the client. List your fee beside the task, and then total the charges. A sample Carpet Cleaning Invoice is included in Appendix B.

Cleaning Carpets

First, start by moving furniture as agreed upon with the client. Pre-treat any heavily soiled or spotted areas, and condition carpets if clients requested it as part of their services.

Complete the carpet cleaning as specified in the contract with the proper equipment, and then replace the furniture. Take care to put a shield, such as foam blocks, between the wet carpet and wood feet of furniture. After the cleaning, suggest clients keep fans or air conditioner units running to circulate air and help with the drying process.

Other Cleaning Services

Before you offer additional services to clients, be sure you are aware of everything these services entail. You can take courses or arrange trainings with equipment vendors to get a feel for what you need to do to make the service a regular offering in your lineup. You can also find books and other media written for specific cleaning chores at your library, bookstore, or on the Internet.

Whatever you offer, know the basics about that service before touting it to customers. Think about these questions before adding a service to your listing:

✓ What can this service offer your clients?

✓ What equipment does it require?

✓ Are their special chemicals or cleaning solutions you will need to use?

✓ How long will the job take you to complete?

✓ Do your employees need specialized training to perform the task?

✓ What is your cost analysis and markup percentage on the service to make a reasonable profit?

✓ How often should it be performed for best results?

Establishing Chemical and Product Inventory

Hundreds of cleaning solutions, solvents, and formulas exist for each job you perform. Put thought into the type of cleaning products you will use before meeting customers so that you knowledgeable about the product.

An easy way to learn about your options is to visit a local janitorial supply store and speak with the employees there. Companies may claim their products are non-toxic and/or biodegradable — a feature that may attract clients — but do the label investigations yourself to be sure what you tell customers is the truth.

Your state may require you to list the contents and toxicity levels of the chemicals in your inventory. Seek out this information — also known as a Materials Safety Data Sheet (MSDS) — from the vendor for each product you are considering purchasing.

Chemical Storage

Buying a large quantity of any cleaning product is unnecessary at the beginning of your business. You can purchase additional product as needed. It makes no sense to waste precious startup cash on inventory you have not yet established a need for.

Buying solutions and cleaners in one-gallon containers or less is a good practice. Keep the cleaners in their original containers with the labels intact. When you put materials into other containers, like spray bottles or misters, be sure to clearly label the container with a permanent marker.

If you have questions on a particular product or want more information, contact your local health and safety office and your insurance agent regarding restrictions on chemical usage as per your policy.

Case Study: Michelle Burnett & Jessie McDonald

You Name It! Home Rescue, LLC

Milford Center, OH

Michelle Burnett and

Jessie McDonald, co-owners

Of all the skills and abilities potential cleaning business owners need to be successful, patience is one of the most important in all aspects of business ownership, according to Michelle Burnett of You Name It! Home Rescue, LLC.

Becoming an established business can take several months or longer. After you are open to servicing clients, developing a following as a trustworthy company can take just as much time. One of the best ways to build a quality reputation is to be up front and honest with clients. Taking the time to determine if you can complete a job the way a customer wants it done and referring the client to other the way a customer wants it to be done and referring the client to other businesses if you do not have the means or skills to do so may result in a smaller profit for you but will build trust.

It is important to take on only as many jobs as you can complete with full attention to quality rather than fill your schedule with tasks for the sake of quantity. It can be frustrating if you have clients contact you for a job beyond your abilities. In the long run, it is better to focus your attention on jobs that you can complete well and that customers will take note of.

If you approach each job with the sense of making the client's home healthy and go the extra mile to make the client happy and comfortable, you will build the reputation as one of the best.

Conclusion

There is so much work that goes into starting, establishing, and growing a successful business that you may be overwhelmed before you even begin. There are challenges to face and mistakes to be made, but trials and tribulations have an uncanny way of giving way to success for those who find their motivation in passion for the job.

There will be opportunities to change your thoughts, your approaches, and your goals. Do this in the thoughtful way that you began your business venture; take time to look at where you need to go, and evaluate what you have done so far. From that, base your decisions on research and a genuine interest in improving your business for not only you, but your clients and employees as well.

Be wary of the notion that after you have your business and services up and running you do not need to make changes. The cleaning industry continually evolves, and keeping up with this will keep your services in demand by clients. From techniques to equipment to products, a close eye on the trends will help you build your reputation as a knowledgeable and competent service provider.

Do not let your focus on your cleaning business diminish your success. Celebrate your achievements — no matter how small — with family, friends, employees, and clients who have supported your quest for business ownership.

You are not just creating a job and source of income for yourself and your family; you are creating a lifestyle and a way of life based on your passion for cleaning and organizing. Be proud of what you do and what you bring to the lives of your customers and employees, and always start each day with the belief, hope, and focus that your services do — and will — make a difference to those around you. Live your dream and live it to the best of your abilities, and you will be the success you dreamed you could be.

Appendix A: Resources

Government Resources

U.S. Small Business Association
(800) U-ASK-SBA (1-800-827-5722)
answerdesk@sba.gov
www.sba.gov

U.S. Patent and Trademark Office
(800)786-9199
usptoinfo@uspto.gov
www.uspto.gov

U.S. Department of Labor
Frances Perkins Building
200 Constitution Avenue, NW
Washington, DC 20210
(866)4-USA-DOL
www.dol.gov

Cleaning Associations

Restoration Industry Association
9810 Patuxent Woods Dr., Suite K
Columbia, MD 21046-1595 USA
(800)272-7012, (443)878-1000
Fax: (443)878-1010
www.ascr.org

Cleaning Equipment Trade Association
1601 North Bond Street, Suite 303
Naperville, IL 60563
(800)441-0111, (630)369-7784
Fax: (630)369-3773
marlene@ceta.org
http://ceta.org/

International Window Cleaners Association
14 W. Third Street, Suite 200
Kansas City, MO 64105
(800) 875-4922
FAX (816) 472-7765
iwca@robstan.com
www.iwca.org/

Professional Carpet and Upholstery Cleaners Association
PO Box 21412
Denver, CO 80221
(877) 4447-2822
info@pcuca.org
www.pcuca.org

Credit Cards

American Express
(800) 492-3344
https://home.americanexpress.com

Discover Card
Discover Financial Services
P.O. Box 30943
Salt Lake City, UT 84130-0943
(800) DISCOVER
www.discovercard.com

Mastercard
(800) 622-7747
www.mastercard.com

Visa
(800) 847-2311
www.Visa.com

PayPal.com
1-888-221-1161
www.paypal.com

Franchise Opportunities

Jani-King International, Inc.
16885 Dallas Parkway
Addison, TX 75001
(800) JANIKING
www.janiking.com

The Maids International
4820 Dodge Street
Omaha, NE 68132
(800) 843-6243
www.maids.com

Molly Maid, Inc.
3948 Ranchero Drive
Ann Arbor, MI 48108
(800)886-6559
www.mollymaid.com

MaidPro Franchising Home Office
180 Canal St.
Boston, MA 02114
(617) 742-8787
http://maidpro.com

The ServiceMaster Company
860 Ridge Lake Boulevard
Memphis, Tennessee 38120
(888) 937-3783
www.servicemaster.com

Trade Publications

Cleanfax Magazine Online
www.cleanfax.com

**Cleaning & Maintenance
Management Online**
www.cmmonline.com

Other Resources

www.score.org
www.cleanlink.com

Appendix B: Worksheets & Checklists

Chapter 1

Necessary Skills for Potential Cleaning Business Owners

On a scale of 1 (least confident) to 10 (most confident), rank your strength in each skill area. If your ranking is 5 or less, note on the line some ideas on how to develop or improve your comfort level (i.e. business courses, research, talking with professionals).

_____ Making important decisions in a short period of time_____

_____

_____ Research skills_____

_____

_____ Sense of responsibility toward clients and employees _____

_____

_____ Knowledge of your niche/specialty _____

_____

_____ Familiarity with fundamental business skills and knowledge _____

_____

_____ Ability to work with demanding people while maintaining professionalism ____

_____

Necessary Skills for Potential Cleaning Business Owners

_____ Multitasking skills _____

_____ Focus to follow through on boring/uninteresting jobs in a timely manner ____

_____ Comfortable assigning tasks and dealing with issues and problems _____

_____ Not afraid of hands-on learning and making mistakes in the learning process

_____ Building relationships and networking social skills_____

_____ Attention to detail _____

_____ Leadership potential _____

_____ Dedication to investing time_____

_____ Basic knowledge of technology and willingness to stay technologically current _____

Chapter 2

Choosing Your Business Type

Use this worksheet to note aspects of each business type to help you choose which ones best suit your needs.

Consumer/Residential/Maid Service

Desirable: Undesirable:

_____   _____

_____   _____

Janitorial Service

Desirable: Undesirable:

_____   _____

_____   _____

Choosing Your Business Type

Franchise

Desirable: Undesirable:

_____   _____

_____   _____

Niche

Desirable: Undesirable:

_____   _____

_____   _____

Chapter 3

Maid Services Checklist

Whole-house

✓ Dusting (furniture, blinds, televisions, and fixtures)

✓ Making beds

✓ Vacuuming floors, drapery, and furniture

✓ Polishing furniture

✓ Scrubbing tubs, showers, sinks, and faucets

✓ Cleaning mirrors, floors, telephones, light switches, and door handles

✓ Removing trash

Kitchen

✓ Wiping down cabinets, countertops, cupboards, appliance exteriors, and microwave interiors

✓ Dusting tops of cabinets

✓ Cleaning countertops and sinks

Optional Services

Whole house

✓ Washing walls and windows

Maid Services Checklist

✓ Changing bed and bath linens

✓ Cleaning fireplaces, windowsills, baseboards, doors, and frames.

✓ Strip, wax, and buff floors

✓ Oil and polish woodwork

Kitchen

✓ Cleaning the refrigerator

✓ Defrosting the freezer

✓ Oven and under-stovetop cleaning

Janitorial Service Checklist

✓ Dusting

✓ Vacuuming

✓ Trash removal

✓ Mopping/wet cleaning

✓ Restroom, lunch room, and common area cleaning

✓ Administrative office cleaning

✓ Floor stripping, waxing, and buffing services

✓ Window cleaning

✓ Carpet shampooing/cleaning

✓ Specialized floor care

What Services Will You Offer?

Read through the types of services you can offer and check the ones you are most interested in offering to clients.

Residential

Maid Services

☐ Single-family homes

☐ Apartments

What Services Will You Offer?

- ☐ Condominiums
- ☐ Rental homes
- ☐ Model homes
- ☐ New builds
- ☐ Common areas in multi-unit buildings
    - ☐ Restrooms
    - ☐ Laundry rooms
    - ☐ Workout rooms
    - ☐ Clubhouses
    - ☐ Meeting rooms

Downsizing Services

- ☐ Organizing possessions
- ☐ Physically moving into new residence
- ☐ Clean new and old residences
- ☐ Waste collection and removal
- ☐ Painting and restoration services
- ☐ Carpet cleaning
- ☐ Packing and unpacking

Estate Cleaning

Seasonal Cleaning

Carpet and Upholstery Cleaning

Commercial

Janitorial Services

- ☐ Offices
- ☐ Warehouses
- ☐ Restaurants

What Services Will You Offer?

- ☐ Coffee Shops
- ☐ Urgent Care Facilities
- ☐ Doctor's Offices
- ☐ Dentist's Offices
- ☐ Food Services
- ☐ Apartment Common Areas

Disaster Cleaning/Restoration

Window & Blind Cleaning

Ceiling and Wall Cleaning

Other Miscellaneous Services

Chapter 4

Creating a Successful Business Name

1. What type of business are you planning? _____
_____

2. What images do you want to create in the customer's mind when they hear your business name? _____
_____

3. What feelings, emotions or benefits will your services provide clients? _____
_____

4. Are there any special details, such as your geographic area, a nickname, a word, number or phrase, a specific service, or specialty you would like to incorporate in your name?_____
_____

5. Set aside a time to brainstorm name ideas. Using your responses, mix and match possibilities. Do not censor yourself during this session. Write down all possibilities; then take time away from the list to clear your head. Work backwards from your list, crossing out names you are sure you do not want to use to discover the names you like until you make your choice.

Business Plan Outline

Section 1

Introduction
- Cover Page
- Table of Contents
- Vision Statement

Section 2

Business Summary
- Mission Statement
- Goals
- Operations
- Inventory
- Startup Timetable

Organizational Plan
- Company Management Structure
- Staffing Needs
- Staffing Procedure
- Consultants and Advisors
- Legal Structure
- License and Permit Information

Marketing Strategy
- Ideal Customer
- Ideal Markets
- Business Location and Analysis
- Promotional and Marketing Plan

Financial Plan
- Startup Funding Sources
- Location Needs
- Equipment Needs
- Insurance and Bonding Details
  - Sample Statements
  - Balance Sheet
  - Profits and Losses
  - Personal Financial Statements
  - Personal Federal Income Tax Returns
  - Break Even Analysis
- Projected Information
  - Three-year cash flow statement
  - Worst-case income and cash flow statement

Business Plan Outline

Section 3

Conclusion
- Business Plan Summary
- Appendices of important documents
  - Market Research Studies
  - Sample Advertisements
  - Lease/rental Information
  - Licensing Documents

Creating Your Vision Statement

A vision statement is the "big idea" of your company. It is the guiding image you want your company to reflect in society. Using these questions, create a vision statement unique to your business.

1. What three values are your business based upon?

    1. _____

    2. _____

    3. _____

2. What are the three most important goals of your business?

    1. _____

    2. _____

    3. _____

3. What three things do you most want to provide for your clients?

    1. _____

    2. _____

    3. _____

4. Where do you see your business in three to five years? _____
_____

5. Using these responses, think about these in creating your vision statement:

    a. What do you believe your business can become in the future?

    b. How would you define the dream you hold for your company?

    c. What does your company stand for?

Creating Your Vision Statement

d. How will you determine your company's success in non-monetary terms?

e. What images come to mind when you envision your company's success?

6. Write your vision statement as a specific, factual representation of where you want your business to be. For example:

a. Kanisha's Cleaning strives to be the leader in integrity, reliability and personal customer service.

b. Green Clean Janitorial Services offers the most thorough cleaning services in Howard County.

c. M.A. Steam Cleaning provides quality carpet cleaning services to improve the homes and health of every client.

Creating Your Mission Statement

A mission statement defines how your company will take action to achieve your vision statement. It is clear, compelling, and inspires others into doing. Using these questions, create a mission statement unique to your business.

1. What are the three main purposes of your business?

1. _____

2. _____

3. _____

2. What are the three to five main services your business offers clients?

1. _____

2. _____

3. _____

3. What values are important to your business? (from the Vision statement worksheet if you like) _____

_____

4. What top three problems do you want to solve for your customers?

1. _____

2. _____

3. _____

Creating Your Mission Statement

5. Using these responses, think about these in creating your mission statement:

   a. How will you fulfill the needs of your customers?

   b. What actions are required of your employees to meet this need?

   c. How will you determine your company's success in non-monetary terms?

   d. What images come to mind when you envision your company's success?

6. Write your mission statement in a motivational phrase. For example:

   a. Kanisha's Cleaning provides maid and personal errand service with a smile.

   b. M.A. Steam Cleaning provides quality carpet cleaning services to improve the homes and health of every client.

Chapter 5

Quarterly Cash Flow

Month/Year				
	Estimated	**Actual**	Estimated	**Actual**
Income				
Sales				
Savings				
Loans				
Startup				
Miscellaneous				
Total Income				
Expenditures				
Rent				
Utilities				
Telephone				
Labor				
Insurance				
Office Supplies				
Products				
Licenses				

Quarterly Cash Flow

Advertising				
Postage				
Miscellaneous				
Fixtures				
Maintenance				
Interest				
Total Expenditures				
Total Income (minus)				
Total Expenditures				
Balance Forward				

Profit and Loss (Income) Statement

Sample Monthly Income Statement for the Month Ending:

Income:

Cleaning Services	0.00
Expenses	0.00
Wages	0.00
Advertising	0.00
Products	0.00
Repairs	0.00
Insurance	0.00
Depreciation	0.00
Interest	0.00
Supplies	0.00
Total Expenses	0.00
Net Income	0.00

Income Record

Client	Date Billed	Amount Due	Date Paid	Comments/Notes

Bi-Annual Expense Record (First Six Months)

	Jan.	Feb.	March	April	May	June
Service						
Supplies						
Equipment						
Insurance						
Bonding						
Advertising						
Transportation						
Professional Services						
Office Expenses						
Supplies						
Telephone						
Cell Phone						
Internet						
Other Expenses						
Total Expenses						

Bi-Annual Expense Record (Second Six Months)

	July	Aug.	Sept.	Oct.	Nov.	Dec.
Service						
Supplies						
Equipment						
Insurance						
Bonding						
Advertising						

Bi-Annual Expense Record (Second Six Months)						
	July	Aug.	Sept.	Oct.	Nov.	Dec.
Transportation						
Professional Services						
Office Expenses						
Supplies						
Telephone						
Cell Phone						
Internet						
Other Expenses						
Total Expenses						

Chapter 7

Pay Rate Scale Research

Directions: Using the Yellow Pages, Chamber of Commerce listings and the internet, list the names of cleaning companies in your area and their phone number. Contact them to find out their minimum and maximum rates of pay and their pay rates for individual positions if possible. Use these figures to determine pay rates for your company.

Business Name & Number _____

Minimum and Maximum Pay Rates _____

Entry Level Rate: _____

Previous Experience Rate: _____

Crew Supervisor Rate: _____

Secretarial/Office Staff Rate: _____

Marketing/Advertising Staff Rate: _____

Other Rate: _____

Sample Interview Questions

Applicant Name_____

Interview Date_____

1. Why did you apply for this job?

2. What skills, talents or abilities do you bring to this job that would make you the best choice?

3. What are your goals for your career? Your life?

4. What experience do you have cleaning?

5. What do you think are your three strongest character traits?

6. Do you like working alone? Why or why not?

7. Do you like working with a team or crew? Why or why not?

8. What can you add to our company?

9. How important are schedules?

10. How well do you work with schedules?

11. Is this a second or a primary job for you?

12. Why do you think confidentiality is important to this business?

13. What is your definition of clean?

14. How would you react if:

    a. You saw another employee looking through a client's dresser or desk?

    b. You accidentally broke something in a client's home?

    c. A client wanted to talk to you while you were cleaning?

    d. You woke up and did not feel like coming to work?

    e. You felt you had too much work to do and you were not getting support from your crewmembers?

    f. You could not complete a job in the time you were supposed to finish?

15. How do you see yourself fitting into this company?

16. What questions do you have about the company or the position?

Post Interview Notes

To be used following an interview to record impressions, insight and details about applicants.

Responses to Interview Questions

Notes:_____
_____

Personal Grooming/Dress

Notes:_____
_____

Manners, Mannerisms, Behavior

Notes:_____
_____

Interpersonal Skills

Notes:_____
_____

Positive Impressions

Notes:_____
_____

Areas of Concern

Notes:_____
_____

Hiring Process Checklist

Applicant Name: _____

Date Application Received: _____ Date contacted for interview: _____

Date Interviewed: _____

Results of Interview: Hired   Not Hired

Notes from Interview: _____
_____

Date notified of result: _____ Date employee contract signed: _____

Youth Work Log

Employee Name: _____

Month and Year: _____

Date: _____

Jobs Performed: _____

Starting Time: _____

Ending Time: _____

Total Time: _____

Weekly Hours: _____

Monthly Hours: _____

Application Form

Applicant Information

Name: _____

Address: _____

Phone/Cellphone: _____

E-mail: _____

Where did you hear about our company? _____

Experience

What experience do you have cleaning offices or homes? _____
_____

Previous Employment

Employer: _____

Address: _____

Phone: _____

E-mail: _____

Dates employed _____ to _____

Reason for leaving: _____

Application Form

Position/Job Description: _____

Salary/Pay Rate: _____

References

Please give the names and contact information for three non-family members who can provide details about your work abilities and skills

Name: _____

Employer: _____

Address: _____

Phone: _____

E-mail: _____

Relationship: _____

Name: _____

Employer: _____

Address: _____

Phone: _____

E-mail: _____

Relationship: _____

Name: _____

Employer: _____

Address: _____

Phone: _____

E-mail: _____

Relationship: _____

Application Form

Employment

Temporary _____

Part-Time_____

Full-Time_____

What days and hours are you available to work?_____
_____

What days are best for you to come in for an interview?_____

If selected for a position, when can you start?_____

Can you work weekends and/or evenings?_____

Do you have transportation to/from work?_____

I verify the information included on this application is true. In the case that I am hired to work for this company, I understand that any false statement provided will be sufficient reason for termination and/or legal action.

Applicant Signature_____

Date_____

Training Planning Session

Training Focus: _____

Orientation: _____

Service Techniques: _____

Professional Development: _____

Training Date: _____

Training Location: _____

Training Hours: _____

Lunch Provided: _____ Lunch on your own _____

Training Objectives: _____
_____

Training Activities to Achieve Goals: _____ Lecture _____ Worksheets
_____ Hands-On _____ Group Work _____ Demonstration

Training Planning Session

Scenarios to Incorporate: _____

Presenter(s): _____

Materials Needed: _____

Evaulation of Learning: _____

Employee Handbook

Section 1: Daily Operations and Expectations

Job Descriptions
   Crew worker/cleaner
   Crew supervisor/chief
   Secretary/Office specialist
   Marketing/Advertising specialist
   Owner/President/CEO
Who to Contact for Employment Issues
   Upcoming Job Schedules
   Scheduling Time Off
   Calling in Sick
   Late Arrival
   General Problems and Issues

Section 2: Dress Code

What to Wear: Non-Uniform
    Shirts
    Pants
    Shoes
    Other
What to Wear: Uniform
    Policies and Expectations
    Replacement Policy

Section 3: Company Policies

Work Hours and Lunch Breaks
Disciplinary Policies for Breaking Rules
Requesting Vacation Time/Time Off
Suspected Theft
Unsatisfactory Performance
Evaluation and Promotion Procedures

Chapter 8

Image and Logo Planning

What pictures or images do you think best represent your services? _____
_____

Which words or phrases represent what you provide to clients? _____
_____

What colors signify fresh and clean to you? _____
_____

What images do you get with these colors? _____
_____

What colors signify energy to you? _____
_____

What images do you get with these colors? _____
_____

What colors signify peace and calm to you? _____
_____

What images do you get with these colors? _____
_____

What is the main feeling you want customers to associate with your business? _____
_____

What images, words/phrases, and colors represent that feeling? _____
_____

Business Trade Show Sales Lead/Contest Entry Form

Name: _____

Company Name: _____

Type of Business: _____

Business Address: _____

Business Phone Number: _____

# of employees: _____

Business Trade Show Sales Lead/Contest Entry Form

Does your company currently have a janitorial/cleaning service? _____

What services do they perform for you? _____

Are there additional services you would like? _____

Who can we contact to discuss janitorial services and your business?

Name: _____

Title: _____

Phone Number: _____

E-mail address: _____

Consumer Trade Show Sales Lead/Contest Entry

Name: _____

Address: _____

Phone Number: _____

Do you live in a/an (circle one): single family home   apartment   condo

What is the approximate square footage of your home/apartment/condo? _____

Do you (circle one)   own   rent

Why are you interested in a cleaning service? _____

Which services would you be interested in finding more about? (circle all that apply)

Housecleaning   Seasonal cleaning   Floor & window cleaning

Moving in/moving out   Other: _____

Domain Name Research

Using an Internet Search Engine, search companies that offer domain names for sale and use this sheet to determine the one that best meets the needs of your business.

Name Provider	Length of Contract	Customer Service	Cost(s)
_____	_____	_____	_____
_____	_____	_____	_____

Web Host Research

Using an Internet Search Engine, search companies that offer domain names for sale, and use this sheet to determine the one that best meets the needs of your business.

Web Host _____

Cost _____

Options & Tools _____

Space _____

Length of Contract _____

Chapter 9

Residential Client Information Form

Home   Apartment   Condo   Other

Name _____

Address _____

Home Phone _____

Work Phone _____

Cell Phone _____

Emergency Number _____

Square Footage _____

Number of levels/floors _____

Number of bedrooms _____

Number of bathrooms _____

Number of living/family spaces _____

Pets   Yes   No   Type _____

Children Yes   No   how many _____   Ages _____

Home Security System?   Yes   No   Code _____

Residential Client Information Form

Home security instructions and contact _____

_____

Received customer key (date)_____

Returned customer key (date)_____

Commercial Client Information Form

Office _____

Business _____

Warehouse _____

Complex _____

Other _____

Name _____

Address _____

Work Phone_____

Cell Phone_____

Emergency Number_____

Square Footage _____

Number of levels/floors_____

Frequency of services requested: daily/nightly   weekly   monthly   other

Security System?   Yes   No   Code_____

Security instructions and contact _____

_____

Received customer key (date)_____

Returned customer key (date)_____

Residential Quote Form

Date: _____ Estimator: _____

Client Name: _____

Address: _____

Phone: _____ Fax: _____

Service Type Requested: Weekly   Bi-Weekly   Monthly   Other

Days and Times to Schedule: _____

House   Apartment   Condo   Other   Square Footage: _____

Services Requested:

Bedrooms: _____

Service	Time needed and/or special instructions
_____ Dusting	Details: _____
_____ Vacuuming	Details: _____
_____ Windows	Details: _____
_____ Blinds/Drapes	Details: _____
_____ Make beds	Details: _____
_____ Desks/Furniture	Details: _____
_____ Garbage Removal	Details: _____
_____ Other	Details: _____
Bathrooms	
_____ Dusting	Details: _____
_____ Tub & Shower	Details: _____
_____ Sinks	Details: _____
_____ Walls	Details: _____
_____ Countertops	Details: _____
_____ Mirrors	Details: _____
_____ Furniture	Details: _____
_____ Windows	Details: _____
_____ Garbage	Details: _____
_____ Mop	Details: _____
_____ Other	Details: _____
Other General Rooms	
_____ Dusting	Details: _____
_____ Vacuuming	Details: _____
_____ Windows	Details: _____
_____ Blinds/Drapes	Details: _____

Residential Quote Form

_____ Desks/Furniture	Details: _____
_____ Garbage Removal	Details: _____
_____ Appliances	Details: _____
_____ Equipment	Details: _____
_____ Mopping	Details: _____

Kitchen

_____ Dusting	Details: _____
_____ Vacuuming	Details: _____
_____ Windows	Details: _____
_____ Blinds/Drapes	Details: _____
_____ Garbage Removal	Details: _____
_____ Fridge/Stove	Details: _____
_____ Small Appliances	Details: _____
_____ Dishwasher	Details: _____
_____ Countertops	Details: _____
_____ Cabinets	Details: _____
_____ Sink	Details: _____
_____ Mop	Details: _____

Stairways

_____ Dust	Details: _____
_____ Vacuum	Details: _____
_____ Polish	Details: _____
_____ Walls	Details: _____

Estimated Hours_____   Rate per hour: _____

Equipment Surcharge: _____   Payment Method: _____

Janitorial Estimate Form

Date: _____   Estimator: _____

Client Name: _____

Address: _____

Phone: _____   Fax: _____

Service Type Requested: Daily   Nightly   Weekly   Monthly

Days and Times to Schedule: _____

Services Requested:

Janitorial Estimate Form

Office Areas

_____ Dusting	Details: _____
_____ Desks/Cabinets	Details: _____
_____ Stairs/Hallways	Details: _____
_____ Water Fountains	Details: _____
_____ Vacuuming	Details: _____
_____ Windows	Details: _____
_____ Blinds/Drapes	Details: _____
_____ Restrooms Cleaned	Details: _____
_____ Garbage Removal	Details: _____
_____ Mopping	Details: _____
_____ Floors Waxed	Details: _____
_____ Other	Details: _____

Common Areas

_____ Dusting	Details: _____
_____ Garbage Removal	Details: _____
_____ Fridge/Stove	Details: _____
_____ Walls	Details: _____
_____ Countertops	Details: _____
_____ Furniture/Appliances	Details: _____
_____ Restrooms	Details: _____
_____ Other	Details: _____

Estimated Hours: _____   Rate per hour: _____

Total Estimate: _____

Janitorial Bidding/Proposal Form

Date: _____

Company Contact: _____

Address: _____

Phone: _____ Fax: _____

Company Name (if different): _____

In response to the requested bid, we submit details and estimates below: _____
_____

Proposed material and labor costs for these estimates: _____

Signature: _____

Janitorial Bidding/Proposal Form

Proposal Accepted_____

The proposed services, prices, specifications and conditions are satisfactory. Upon signature, you are awarded the contract and authorized to begin work as specified in this document. Payment terms will reflect terms and conditions above.

Date_____Signature_____

Date_____Signature_____

Client Handbook

Cover Page

- Complete business name

- Your name

- Mailing address

- E-mail address

- Web site address

- Contact numbers: Phone, cell, pager, fax

- Services offered: one or two lines about the types of services you offer

- Service area: one or two lines of the geographic area your business serves

Table of Contents (if desired)

Mission and Vision Statements

Consultation Process

- From start to finish, how clients can expect you to interact to their request for a cleaning consultation

Services Offered

- Base rates (if desired)

- Services not offered (if desired)

Company Policies

- Cancellation and rescheduling

Client Handbook

- Late arrival of cleaning crew

- Inability to service client's location

- Who provides cleaning products and solutions

- Client/employee interaction

- Scheduling process

- Safety and security procedures

  - Client safety

  - Employee safety

- Billing and payment procedures

- Payment terms

- Payment types

- Late penalties and other fees

- Billing cycle

- Billing process

- Receipts

Contract

  - Standard length

  - Renewal terms

  - Changes in terms

  - Termination

Chapter 10

Markup Percentage Formulas

Formula for Percent Markup

(Selling price) - (actual cost) =d ollar markup
(Dollar markup) / (actual cost) = percentage markup

Markup Percentage Formulas

Samples:

Cleaning Carpet

($200 selling price) – ($150 actual cost) = dollar markup of $50
Percentage markup = $50 dollar markup / $150 actual cost = 33% markup percentage

Cleaning Per Job
($15 selling price) - ($10 actual cost) = dollar markup of $5
Percentage markup = $5 dollar markup / $10 actual cost = 50% markup percentage

Chapter 11

Checklist of Residential Services

Client name: _____

Address: _____

Days serviced: _____

Bedroom Cleaning Checklist

Task	Completed By	Date	Notes
Dusting			
Vacuum			
Windows			
Blinds/Drapes			
Make Bed			
Desks/Furniture			
Garbage Removal			
Other			

Bathrooms Cleaning Checklist

Task	Completed By	Date	Notes
Dusting			
Tub & Shower			
Sinks			
Walls			
Countertop			
Mirrors			
Furniture			

Checklist of Residential Services

Tasks	Completed By	Date	Notes
Windows			
Mop			
Garbage Removal			
Other Cleaning Checklist			
Dusting			
Vacuum			
Windows			
Blinds/Drapes			
Desk/Furniture			
Garbage Removal			
Appliances			
Equipment			
Mopping			
Kitchen Cleaning Checklist			
Dust			
Vacuum			
Windows			
Blinds/Drapes			
Garbage Removal			
Fridge/Stove			
Small Appliances			
Dishwasher			
Countertops			
Cabinets			
Sink			
Mop			
Other			
Stairways Cleaning Checklist			
Dust			
Vacuum			
Polish			
Walls			

Checklists of Janitorial Services

Client name: _____

Address: _____

Days serviced: _____

Waiting Room/Public Area Cleaning Checklist

Tasks	Completed By	Date	Notes
Dusting			
Vacuum			
Windows			
Blinds/Drapes			
Desks/Furniture			
Garbage Removal			
Other			

Bathrooms Cleaning Checklist

Dusting			
Vacuum			
Toilets			
Walls			
Sinks/Countertops			
Mirrors			
Furniture			
Windows/Blinds			
Mop			
Garbage Removal			
Other			

Other Offices/Rooms Cleaning Checklist

Dusting			
Vacuum			
Windows			
Blinds/Drapes			
Desks/Furniture			
Garbage Removal			
Appliances			

Checklists of Janitorial Services			
Tasks	Completed By	Date	Notes
Dusting			
Vacuum			
Windows			
Blinds/Drapes			
Desk/Furniture			
Garbage Removal			
Appliances			
Equipment			
Mopping			
Kitchen/Break Area Cleaning Checklist			
Dusting			
Vacuum			
Windows			
Blinds/Drapes			
Garbage Removal			
Fridge/Stove			
Small Appliances			
Dishwasher			
Countertops			
Cabinets			
Sink/Disposal			
Mop			
Other			
Stairways/Hallways Cleaning Checklist			
Dusting			
Vacuum			
Polish			
Walls			
Other			

Sample Carpet Cleaning Invoice

Business Name: _____

Customer Name: _____

Service Address: _____

City, State, Zip Code: _____

Home Phone: _____

Work Phone: _____

Cell Phone: _____

Date of Estimate: _____

Invoice Number: _____

Technicians: _____

Date and time of service: _____

Areas Cleaned/Services Performed & Amount Due:

_____

_____

_____

_____

_____

Total Amount Due: $_____

Bibliography

Bewsey, S. (2007). *Start and Run a Home Cleaning Business* (3rd ed.). Bellingham, WA: International Self-Counsel Press Ltd.

Entrepreneur Press and Lynn, J. (2006). *Start Your Own Cleaning Service: Your Step-By-Step Guide to Success* (2nd ed.). Entrepreneur Media.

Jorstad, L., & Morse, M. (2006). *How to Start a Home-Based Housecleaning Business* (2nd ed.). Guilford, Connecticut: The Globe Pequot Press.

Author Biography

Beth Morrow, M.Ed., is a freelance author and editor whose credits feature topics such as culture, education, writing, politics, self-help, and gardening. A teacher by trade, she resides in Ohio with her husband, son, and their six-year old black lab.

Index

004295120